Praise for *Second Firsts*

"Second Firsts *will change the way you think about life after loss. With simplicity, science, and raw authenticity, Christina takes you on a journey from a world of loneliness and pain to one of possibilities and action. Her kind and knowledgeable words provide hope and show you that loss can actually inspire the strength and conviction to create the life of your dreams. And her own life stands as a testament to the power of this process.*"

—**Marci Shimoff**, #1 *New York Times* best-selling author of *Love for No Reason* and *Happy for No Reason*

"Second Firsts *is about creating a bigger life after loss. It is about dreaming of a brand-new way to fall in love again with living fully. It is certainly not an easy task, but this little book makes it easier.*"

—**Karen Salmansohn**, best-selling author of *The Prince Harming Syndrome* and *The Bounce Back Book*

"*We can all learn from the wisdom of those who have experienced loss and survived.* Second Firsts *can be your life coach and direct you to heal and create a new life.*"

—**Bernie Siegel, M.D.**, author of *Buddy's Candle* and *365 Prescriptions for the Soul*

"*Christina Rasmussen brilliantly carries the torch for all of those who have suffered loss. She has created the life reentry process th~~~ ~~ll help all people of all ages, and* Second Firsts *will b~ ~~* those who are ready to l~+ ~*

—**Kristine Carlson**, N~ ~ ~ ~ ~'t Sweat the Small Stu~ ~ A Memoir 1~

"*In this moving book, Chri~ ~ ~ ~ both her personal and professional experience with g~~~f to assist those who are suffering to find their way to a new 'normal.' In* Second Firsts *you will discover how to move from merely surviving to once again thriving.*"

—**Anita Moorjani**, *New York Times* best-selling author of *Dying to Be Me*

"If you have experienced loss in your life, Christina's book
will quickly empower you to vibrantly refill, renegotiate, and
embrace your broken-hearted spirit. Please, use your limited time
and energy wisely and seize her Life Reentry program early in your grief.
It will undoubtedly be a big victory for you and the universe.
It's a realistic, strategic, life-shifting, never-look-back program based on
neuroscience and personal experience that leads
you to feeling more genuinely alive
than you ever thought possible."

—**Carolyn Moor**, founder of Modern Widows Club

"Devastating, heartbreaking loss is part of every single life. Christina
has been there herself, and in her book, Second Firsts, she takes your
hand—offering comfort and step-by-step guidance to help you find your
way back into the sunlight. This book will get you living and breathing
again by showing you the way to a joyful, hopeful, and loving life."

—**Paul S. Boyton**, president and CEO of The Moore Center

SECOND
firsts

SECOND
firsts

Live, Laugh,
and Love
Again

Christina Rasmussen

HAY HOUSE, INC.
Carlsbad, California • New York City
London • Sydney • Johannesburg
Vancouver • Hong Kong • New Delhi

Published and distributed in the United States by: Hay House, Inc.: www
.hayhouse.com® • *Published and distributed in Australia by:* Hay House Australia Pty. Ltd.: www.hayhouse.com.au • *Published and distributed in the
United Kingdom by:* Hay House UK, Ltd.: www.hayhouse.co.uk • *Published and
distributed in the Republic of South Africa by:* Hay House SA (Pty), Ltd.: www
.hayhouse.co.za • *Distributed in Canada by:* Raincoast: www.raincoast.com •
Published in India by: Hay House Publishers India: www.hayhouse.co.in

Cover design: Nita Ybarra • *Interior design:* Nick C. Welch

Library of Congress Cataloging-in-Publication Data

Rasmussen, Christina
  Second firsts : live, laugh, and love again / Christina Rasmussen. -- 1st edition.
     pages cm
  Includes bibliographical references.
  ISBN 978-1-4019-4083-6 (pbk. : alk. paper) 1. Bereavement. 2. Adjustment
(Psychology) 3. Change (Psychology). I. Title.
  BF575.G7R37 2013
  155.9'3--dc23
                                      2013017609

Tradepaper ISBN: 978-1-4019-4083-6

16 15 14 13   4 3 2 1
1st edition, November 2013

Printed in the United States of America

To all the unborn Life Starters,
I wrote this book for you

CONTENTS

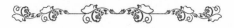

A MESSAGE TO THE READER

I have lived in the shadow of loss—the kind of loss that can paralyze you forever.

I have grieved like a professional mourner—in every waking moment, draining every ounce of my life force.

I died—without leaving my body.

But I came back, and now it's your turn.

I have learned to remember my past—without living in it.

I am strong, electric, and *alive*, because I *chose* to dance, to laugh, to love, and to live again.

I have learned that you can't re-create the life you once had—you have to reinvent a life for yourself.

And that reinvention is a gift, not a curse.

I believe your future self is a work of art and that science can help you create it.

If you're lost . . . if you're gone . . . if you can barely absorb the words on this page . . . I want you to hold this truth in your heart: when it's your time to go, you won't wish you had spent more time grieving; you'll wish you had spent more time living.

That's why I'm here. And why you are, too.

Let's live like our lives depend on it.

INTRODUCTION

I know you are afraid; you are afraid to get hurt again.
But I also know that you are not meant to grieve forever.

Loss is devastating.

It's painful and sad, and it truly stops us in our tracks.

It brings up fears about our safety and abilities.

It makes us question reality. It's so damn unfair. It's literally one of the hardest things we ever face—and we don't get a choice about that.

Because loss is part of being human.

If you've gone through a loss and you're grieving, if you're feeling stuck in the past, if you're trying to put the pieces of your broken life back together, this book is for you. You are more than your loss; you are a whole human being waiting to come back to life. If I were standing before you, I would see the light in your eyes even before you did.

I wrote this book to help you see that light, to see that you have the courage to stand against the fear you are feeling. The clarity to push through the fog you are in.

I wish I could stand next to you right now and comfort you. I'd whisper into your ear that the future is not something to be afraid of. I'd hold your hand and walk you to a safe place where we could sit together and have a conversation. I'd listen and acknowledge your pain.

Then, as we talked, when I sensed you were ready to hear it, I'd share some remarkable information with you that I believe will help you find your way forward.

My mission in life is to help you, and others like you, build a bridge from your past to your future, starting exactly where you are today. You see, before your loss, you were one person. You knew who you were. You made sense in the context of your life. But that identity was ripped away in the moment of your loss. That moment did not only bring pain and sorrow, it also brought confusion and fear. Your brain lost its ability to plan and reason.

This is something that no one can prepare for.

Now you are in an intermediate, transitional phase of your life, where you're waiting to discover the new you—the second you—and find out what your new life will look like. There's a lot of uncertainty at this time. Even though going back to the old life isn't possible, part of you wants to do that anyway. Another part of you wants to go forward—you just don't know how yet.

The secret I want to share with you is that your brain is so adaptive and so powerful that your own thoughts during this painful period can lead you to experience a remarkable, bright future. Even though you are confused and scared, there is a way out of this temporary cloud and onto a powerful bridge. You can help build this bridge to the future, and it can take you wherever you want to go.

This book is just the beginning of a journey you will take with tools you already have but that you have lost during your grief. My role is to guide you through certain steps that will ultimately lead you to an ideal, brand-new lifestyle of your own choosing. I will be your companion throughout the process. I will motivate you and inspire you to take action along the way. I will help you think about what your new life will be by helping you get to know your true self. So then you will know that your new life—which could look a lot like your old life or could be entirely, wildly different—is the best life for you. As you step into this new life, you could take the opportunity to reignite parts of yourself that dimmed because of your loss. You could drop behaviors and attitudes that you don't want to keep. You can take up new hobbies. You can make new friends. Travel to new places. Change your job. Move. Fall in love again. It's your choice. You have a choice to create a new you, so you can experience new firsts—second firsts. Though loss feels painful, you are in control of who you get to be and what happens next.

Of this I am sure: Creating a new lifestyle will require you to change your thoughts and to form new daily habits. Above everything, it will require you to plug in to life day after day after day, no matter how devastating the loss you experienced. How you think, what you do, and the way you participate in life will change your brain and identity, even if only in subtle ways.

The World of Second Firsts

I entered the world of second firsts in September of 1998, when I delivered my master's thesis on the stages of bereavement at the University of Durham in England. But I wasn't thrown into the emotional and practical abyss of needing to create a new beginning for myself until the summer of 2006 when my 35-year-old husband left the physical world. After a devastating and emotionally draining three-year struggle with colon cancer, he passed away, leaving me as a grieving single mother with two young daughters. Nothing I'd been taught or believed about the experience of profound loss was accurate.

I was lost, sad, and very afraid of the future.

This is the book I could have used after I lost my husband. Based on my understanding of the biology of the brain, this book advocates conscious movement through the five stages of a self-guided discovery process that I refer to as the Life Reentry Model. This method was developed from research I have done, my own experience, and the experiences of the thousands of people I have worked with in their quest to overcome grief. It uses the ability of the brain to rewire itself so you are able to move past the fear and sadness that are now ruling your life. Each stage will take you a step closer to moving out of the abyss and into a new life.

While the Life Reentry Model is laid out step by step, reentering life is never a linear process. As you work through these chapters, you'll no doubt want to circle back and reread some of them more than once. The exercises are meant to be used on an ongoing basis; I'll give you periodic reminders of how best to do this. Use the material at your own pace, but stay engaged with the process, as this helps the brain to adapt. Like planting seeds of a future, the Life Reentry Model leads us gradually into the full-blown reality of a new life that can be every bit as rewarding, if not even more fulfilling, than the version of your life that has ended. So get ready for your second firsts.

The second first date.

The second first vacation.

The second first job interview.

The second first *anything* can be hard—and it can also be exciting if it's used to discover new or forgotten parts of your identity. In *Second Firsts*, you'll learn to create the life you want sooner rather than later. This is not easy. But there is a way to deal with starting over that allows for change.

I used the process to change my own life, and it has allowed me to be truly happy again—with a new husband, a new career, and two beautiful new daughters to mother. It has also allowed my private clients and Reentry participants to reclaim their lives. You deserve the same: to be happy and have no regrets that you didn't try. Loss is not something that keeps happening to you; it is an event. You get to decide when you want to step back into life.

START WHERE YOU ARE

If you are in the throes of grief right now, please understand that I won't be asking you to do anything complicated or to move through your grief at a pace that is uncomfortable for you. I am merely asking you to show up every single day and be willing to look at your life and live it, so you may claim that which is yours. If your loss just happened, make sure you take care of yourself as much as possible while reading this book. Self-care and self-love immediately after loss are important for healing. I would also recommend, if your loss just happened, that you read this book, because it will help you feel a tiny glimmer of hope. You may not be ready to do the exercises yet, but it will plant the seed, and you will know that when you are ready to jump-start your life, you can.

This book will be there by your side as a guiding light and companion.

Everyone who has gone through a profound loss has the ability to shift his or her approach to life in such a way that a new life is possible. I am asking you to be open to the opportunities this book will create for you, to engage both your brain and your heart—okay, and a little bit of your imagination. Hope lives there. It lives in the place between reality and the dream world, where everything is possible.

Discovering and building your own new life is up to you. It is never too late . . . or too soon. And you are never too old.

Going forward, I will ask you to put aside any beliefs you may hold about grief and living life after loss. You can live as you grieve, you can move forward when you're scared, and you can shift when you want to stay the same. But I will also ask you to be compassionate and gentle with yourself, to embrace the truth of where you are, and to take time to reflect on both your grief thoughts and life thoughts. When you realize that grief can mean two worlds co-existing—the old and the new—you will start seeing the life that is standing right in front of you.

Some people might argue that, as a society, we don't allow enough time for grief after a loss, but I'd argue that, while it's important to take time to mourn, it's equally important to be able to know when it's time to take action and shift focus from the life we once had to the life we want. While most of the books and research papers I've read on loss point out how the stages of grief are a journey, in reality this journey doesn't end with grief.

Starting over isn't only about the life you left behind. It's about the life that lies ahead of you.

My mission in *Second Firsts* is to deliver the map of a new beginning to you. Starting over after disruptive events that end intimate relationships and throw obstacles in the way of forming new ones is the agenda here.

Please allow me to take you by the hand and be your guide through your second firsts. It is truly my pleasure to be your companion as you start over, learning to live, laugh, and love once again.

Chapter 1

My Second Firsts

I had to see the beauty of my future so I could create it.
I gave airtime to my dreams, and they spoke to me.
I recognized grief's voice and turned the volume down.
Was it easy? No.
Was I scared? Yes.
Did fear get in the way? Heck, no.
And it never will.
My life is worth more than that.
Your life is, too.

I think I know the moment I died.

In the midst of his death, I lost my life, too.

He was just hours away from his last breath, and I was lying next to him on his bed, listening to his heart. Waiting for the inevitable. As his heart was slowing down, my heart was beating faster. *We were both in a place between two worlds.*

In this state of being, one can never go back, despite not yet being released to move forward.

He died on July 21, 2006, at 2:00 A.M.

I died with him, at 2:01 A.M.

His body was lifeless.

My body was numb.

Loss felt like a tsunami hitting me from the inside—my brain, my heart, my arms, my legs—and washing away my inner knowing of what life was supposed to feel like.

There are no words to describe the experience of losing someone you love more than life itself. You cannot know the feeling unless you have experienced it.

My husband of eight years was leaving this world behind. He was in the ICU, dying after battling colon cancer for three and a half years. It felt like I was having an out-of-body experience or watching a movie in slow motion. I wish I knew how it was for him. I wanted to reach out and talk to him. I wanted to ask him what it was like where he was heading.

I wanted to go with him.

But I knew I couldn't. Our one path split in two. It was time to say good-bye. Forever.

The memory of the realization that my life was about to change is imprinted indelibly in my mind. I knew then that the death I felt within me was something I had never been prepared for, and that it was possible I might not survive this powerful kind of grieving.

I was 34 years old, and for the first time in my life, I realized I really knew *nothing* about this kind of pain.

I already missed him, in the few seconds I had been without him.

I remember looking around me, taking in the room.

Watching the darkness, the stillness of the moment.

Everyone else had left the room to give us the privacy to say good-bye. As I was sitting right next to him, time *stopped*. I looked at him.

And then I took my first breath of this new life.

Gasping for air, I got up from the bed. My body did not feel like my own. It was heavy, and tired, and acted as if it did not want to go where I was taking it. But I took it anyway. So there it was: the beginning of a new life, introduced to me at my rock bottom.

Emotionally tormented, mentally deranged from the grief, brokenhearted, and above all else, in love with a dead man, I had begun my new life.

It had happened.

He had died.

Forever.

The silence I experienced that early morning had a physical manifestation. The silence of grief attacks your body. It makes its mark. It is so heavy that it is almost like life slows down until everything pauses. Every time you move and every time you speak, the silence is amplified.

I never knew that silence was so loud during grief.

It was screaming at me.

It was speaking to me, but I could not hear it. I felt insane. I felt unequipped to embrace the new life that was waiting for me to begin to live it.

What I experienced upon my husband's immediate absence was disbelief. I couldn't believe I'd never see him again. I was even questioning whether my husband was dead. Though I had studied the stages of grief, I'd never understood grief of this magnitude, and the finality of death. I questioned death in my mind. I could not understand how he could never come back. I was a human being experiencing an inhuman condition.

Grief.

I remember the water running in the shower. It was so loud. Even water felt painful.

The pain I was experiencing . . . my body truly could not endure that kind of experience for long.

Nobody could help me.

Nobody could help me.

Nobody had warned me that I wouldn't be able to go back to what I had left behind. Not only was he gone, but nothing in my life felt the same.

Everything about me changed, and everything about the world around me was altered forever.

What I did not know then was this: *my new life had nothing to do with the old one.*

My Daughters' Grief

I could not have been more present than when I opened the door to my kids' grief. As a mother, you want to protect your children from anything that could harm them. Yet here I was, entering the house after days away, days of waiting for death to come and take my husband, needing to tell my children that Daddy was no longer with us. I hoped to strike a magical balance between helping them and letting go of my composure and breaking down.

As I stepped inside the front door, my six-year-old daughter raced toward me and leapt jubilantly into my arms. "Mommy, Mommy, you're home!" she shouted. Then, suddenly, the reason for my being home dawned on her. Her face went from bliss to darkness, as she remembered what I had told her two days before, when I took her and her sister to the hospital: Daddy was dying. She went quiet and started crying. This was not a child's cry, but an adult's cry coming from inside a little girl's body.

I have no words to describe how painful it was to see my six-year-old daughter mourning like an adult.

And there was nothing anybody could do to make her feel better.

People say children are resilient and can overcome anything, but I understood that my daughter needed to rely upon my strength. The little strength that I had.

I wished for time to stop, and then for it to speed up and take us years into the future when the pain would have subsided. But yet again, I was asking for the impossible.

My daughter aged years during those next few moments, and I could see that her heart ached with the knowledge of something so unbearable.

A few moments later, my four-year-old raced out of her room. Like her sister, she was very happy to see me come home. But I knew our conversation would be different, as she was so much younger. I picked her up and carried her back to bed so we could cuddle.

As we were sitting on her bed hugging, I told my daughter that Daddy was no longer going to be living with us, that he had just died. I also told her that he'd be watching over us. She started to think about this and went quiet for a while. I sat patiently on her bed waiting for her to say something. She looked at me and said, "Mommy, since Daddy is watching over us every day, does that also mean he can see all the things that I'm doing?"

I burst into laughter in the midst of the worst day of my life. I couldn't believe how her child's mind was processing this difficult event. She was concerned that she could no longer be naughty behind my back, since her daddy was now everywhere.

Instead of trying to get her to understand the importance of that day, I responded, "That's right, honey. He can see everything you're doing."

I learned so much from that moment. I learned that laughter could still walk into our lives when we least expected it.

I didn't break down while I was telling my girls about their father, and it wasn't because I was trying to be strong; mostly it was because everything inside me was frozen and there was nothing I could do to melt the grief away. I had already been broken into so many pieces that I couldn't imagine anything would ever put me back together.

FOOD FOR GRIEF

I never could have predicted what my introduction to the outside world of grief would look like. What I saw, through my freshly bereaved eyes, was not overwhelming or catastrophic, but it was unexpected: a sea of sad faces surrounding me as they uttered the same words over and over again.

"I am so sorry, Christina."

"I am so sorry, Christina."

"We can cook dinner for you if you need us to."

"We are here. If you need anything, just let us know."

"I can make macaroni and cheese for the kids, just say the word."

The casseroles kept coming. Every couple of days, there was a different dish on the menu of grief. Some of these dishes were so beautifully prepared, and had so much sentiment poured into them, that I remember feeling tremendously loved and taken care of. My girls were excited every day to see what was for dinner. I just wished those casseroles could feed me life, hope, and a hug in

the lonely nights. I was scared to death and suffocating every waking moment.

The last thing I wanted to think about was food.

I had forgotten how to eat. Smelling food made me nauseous.

Everything tasted like nothing. I wanted to scream my truth to the world, grab people by the arms and shake them with my grief. I wanted to wake them up and tell them I had also died. It felt like I was talking to the deaf and the blind. They all seemed to use the same words to console me. "Just take one day at a time, Christina."

Didn't they know that every day felt like a whole year, every moment was like a knife stab in my heart? I felt like I was living a heartless life. I was introduced to the robotic and plastic nature of the world's reaction to pain and sorrow. Everyone could see my pain, but they could only imagine its gigantic presence.

I didn't blame them; my friends and family could only do so much. They were all young, and they had never experienced such tragedy. Their husbands, wives, girlfriends, boyfriends, and children were all there, by their side. I could already hear my bitterness.

I was bitter for everyone else having what I had just lost, the love of my life.

I am ashamed to admit it, but I hated their happiness. I despised their perfect lives.

I could not recognize myself. My terrible thoughts could not possibly be mine. These people loved me, and I loved them back. Where was this coming from?

You see, I lived close to caring and loving folks who wanted to help us, yet they didn't know how, unless they were asked to cook or bake something. Trust me, they wanted to do more, but they also knew that nothing they did would be enough. I knew no one could help me escape the terrible unending pain of my loss. I also felt guilty for my jealousy toward their happiness. I just wanted to go back to the nice Christina with the perfect life.

I wanted to go back to my love, back to the happy life I had just exited.

I wanted to do the impossible.

The way out of this pain was a big mystery to me. I would wake up in the morning and forget what had happened for a split second, only to remember with such cruelty and torture. I wanted to tell everyone about my very broken heart. Sometimes I tried. But I remained frozen in pain, with no tears coming out.

Some people didn't even say much to me when I told them that my 35-year-old husband had just died. Others broke down and cried. I felt I had no choice except to put my arms around them and tell them it was going to be okay. They were grieving my grief, mourning my loss, so I somehow found myself being strong for them. It was easier to help others in the midst of my grief than to help myself. My tragic life brought people to tears wherever I went, so even people I'd never met before would approach me and say, much like all the others, that they were sorry.

After the loss of my husband, I believed time would heal me. I listened to all the people who brought me food for months, who told me to just wait, to give it some time.

This too shall pass.

And I believed that.

I wholeheartedly trusted that after a specific duration of time, things in my life would fall back into place. I'd been told "Time heals all wounds" too many times to count, and my brain came to accept this statement as the truth. So I entered into a waiting period, a period of

waking up morning after morning, hoping I would feel better than the day before.

I felt as if I were on fire and nobody would or could put it out. Every day, everywhere I went and in everything I did, I was burning hot, and everyone around me kept telling me that I needed to wait patiently for that fire to go out. But the heat of loss was agonizing.

You see, I loved my husband more than I loved life itself. The pain of losing him was an unbearable force. I felt my heart dying slowly. I sensed my body aging quickly. Worse yet, I went numb. I stopped feeling emotions, and this robbed me of my tears of sadness. I wanted to cry, to purge my sorrow, but I couldn't. I felt guilty for not being able to cry.

I was angry that nobody had told me how bad this was going to feel.

Why hadn't the world prepared me for this agony?

He had been dying for more than three years. How come nobody told me that I was to die with him?

I was on a roller-coaster ride that wouldn't end, and I had no idea how to get off.

THE PRACTICAL SIDE OF MY LOSS

I wish there was only the emotional world of grief to face, but there is another world that grief takes ahold of and never wants to let go. There is a part of life that does not stop to wait for you to feel better.

Kids have to go to school.

Dinner must get prepared every night.

Money needs to be earned.

That is the duality of loss, when the world inside no longer matches the world outside.

That is when you break in half, trying to match the internal with the external.

The good news and the bad news is that I come from a family that stands by you when something grave happens. They want to take on your pain, your everyday chores, your motherly duties, and your life. I knew this and understood it as an expression of how much they cared about me, but I didn't want it. I felt it would be better for my long-term recovery if I grieved alone and, from a practical perspective, made it through the transition without anybody taking my responsibilities away. Otherwise I felt as if my grief would last forever.

After a couple of weeks, during which my parents moved into my house to help me and my girls, I told them, "I have to do this on my own." I must have looked determined, as they listened to me and left soon after. They knew to trust me with this important decision.

This is not to say I didn't need any help. I did. But I felt that the more others helped me with the practical matters of life, the longer it would take me to find my way back to happiness. My plan was to figure things out by myself. I passionately wanted to stand on my own two feet. This meant going back to school, getting a job, and raising my kids on my own. I knew I definitely would face challenges.

There were many days when I surrendered to grief. I was sad and lonely, and I missed my husband. I'm not going to lie to you about that. But other times, I felt like grief and I were fighting each other. At those times, grief didn't win.

I didn't know it then, but it was significant that I was not willing to take grief lying down. If I'm being honest, I was not standing up straight, either. But I was not

defeated. I stayed focused on the future as best I could, even if for only a few minutes a day. I wanted to survive grief by acquiring new skills, a new attitude, and a new life. And I did.

Gradually, over the next couple of years, I was able to transform my sorrow into the fuel that would launch me into a new life of passion and creation. But this didn't happen overnight. In fact, the first glimpse I had of a life without sadness or not solely defined by my loss came many months after my husband died.

Before I get into that story, I want you to imagine that my life at the time was like the movie *Groundhog Day*, where the same day is being lived over and over again. I would wake up, drop the kids off at school, go to work, pick up the kids at night, prepare and eat dinner, go to bed . . . and then it would start over again. I was physically and emotionally exhausted. When you are in a tunnel of grief like this, you can't see the light at the other end. Grief is relentless, and it feels as though there is no way out. So you just hang on and cycle through your days and their sameness.

During the week leading up to my second Christmas without my husband, a year and a half after he passed away, the mail carrier kept driving past my house every day without delivering my mail, which included all of my precious Christmas cards. I realized that this was because there was snow on the ground and not much space for him to park his mail truck, so I woke up on a sunny Saturday morning and shoveled the snow away from the mailbox. I was really looking forward to reading those cards.

To my surprise, even after all my hard work, the mail-man did not stop. You can imagine the disappointment

I felt after shoveling for two hours! I was furious. The fire that loss had ignited within my body was burning up. But instead of sitting down on my couch and crying endlessly, I put on my snow boots and jacket and started running as fast as I could down the road to catch up with him. I must have looked like one very crazy woman. I don't believe my neighbors ever quite saw me in the same way after my running episode.

Finally I caught up with the mail truck and, completely out of breath, asked the mailman, "May I please have my mail?"

He handed it to me and then mumbled, "Why don't you ask your husband to shovel a little better?"

It was almost as if this sentence was supposed to be delivered to me at that point in time. I mean, who says that? It's incredibly rude. But this man did. He said that sentence to me.

With a straight face, holding back my tears and showing as much strength as I could muster, I replied, "He would if he could, but he's dead." Then I walked away with my mail, feeling victorious. I did not even wait to see if his face was turning red.

That day I decided I was no longer going to allow grief to keep me passive. I was no longer going to just accept what was happening to me. Not accepting the mail carrier passing my house brought me closer to not accepting my life as it had become: sad, sorrowful, and pitiful, spending Christmas alone with my little girls, thousands of miles away from our other family members.

Before that decision, the picture of my life was that I was all by myself, feeling like a pathetic victim with nobody helping me out. Even the mailman was not delivering my Christmas cards. You can see it, right?

After that decision, everything changed. I started to see the light more and more. I began to have the strength to go proudly after what was mine.

My mail became a metaphor for my life.

SHOWING UP

Before my crazy quest to get my mail, I thought I'd done everything in my power to jump-start my life: I had gone back to school, I had taken my girls on weekend trips, I had even found a great job. Yet I was suffering day in and day out. Grief was still a protagonist in my life story. Then something new began pushing me forward: my desperation and thirst for life!

Was it easy for me when I was chasing the mail truck, my feet pounding hard on the frozen snow, breathless and desperate to catch up? No. It was uncomfortable and very unlike me. But after this uncharacteristic event, I realized I had a power I wasn't familiar with, and its origins were somewhere in the deeply emotional journey I had taken since my husband died.

As my grief started transforming into a source of unlimited power, I was able to begin to focus my attention and take my life in a new direction. After Christmas, I went back to work with a new attitude. I returned to my routine more hopeful about my future prospects. This had nothing to do with anything other than a shift of perspective. My colleagues at work kept asking me if something was different in my life, as I seemed happier. I couldn't possibly explain to them all that I'm describing here, as this was too much for a five-minute conversation, and it was certainly not something they could really grasp unless they'd been privy to my journey.

Glimpses of what my life could become began materializing before my eyes. Three weeks later, I applied for a much bigger job within my company and I got it! People started behaving differently toward me; it was as if they could see Christina again. Before that, my grief had made me act like a paler version of myself, someone nearly invisible. Grief not only made me invisible to others, it also demanded a bigger loss, the loss of my true essence. It wasn't that my grief was a villain, but it robbed me of my power and created a huge vacuum in my life that had to be filled with a new identity—one with which I was not yet familiar.

When I saw my own potential and that I was not like everyone else anymore, I started asking for things I wanted. A key difference now was that I also felt I deserved to receive them. I saw myself as someone with magnificent strength and a fearless attitude. After all, I had been to hell and back. What was there to lose? Not much!

I interviewed for the new job with a man who held one of the highest-ranking positions in my company. He said something to me that I would only come to understand later: "Christina, you may not have the practical experience to do this job, but you do have personal experience that will provide you with the skills you need and much more. That's why you had the job before you even entered my office."

Soon after my promotion, I planned a party for all of the friends who had stuck by me during the previous year and a half, when I had been absent and unavailable. I wanted to thank them and invite them back into my life so we could renew our friendships.

Twenty days into the new year, I went out on a first date with my future husband, and my heart started beating a little faster again. If I hadn't taken the steps toward rebuilding my own life, reclaiming what was always mine, and getting to know the stronger me, I would not have been in the position to receive his love when we met.

I earned my results. I earned the personal and professional growth that followed my loss. I showed up, and then showed up some more, until I finally managed to stand up straight and demonstrate to the world the new person I had become. I showed up for my mail, for my life, for my job, and for my kids . . . and as I did, little by little, grief started to move away from me.

I can tell you it was not easy. It's actually harder to live and grieve than just to grieve. But I believe the difficulty was worth it.

Yes, it is hard to get up and put on your boots and start chasing a truck down the street. It would have been much easier for me just to sit at home and feel sorry for myself. But I chose to do the complete opposite. If you are thinking that what I did that snowy day was a simple, basic thing, you're right: That is the truth. But only part of it.

There is so much inherent power in loss, power that can be used as an unlimited source of fuel to set yourself into motion so you can start the process of rebuilding your life. The reason I was running behind the mail carrier as fast as I could wasn't because I was particularly fit or a runner. Grief was making me run like this. It gave me the determination to go and get my mail!

It was important for me to come to the realization, when I was ready, that *enough is enough, and I am not going to do this anymore.* I had to stand up and take charge of my entire life—not just the day-to-day practicalities of it.

Grief Is a Portal

It took me a little longer to realize that my grief was a gateway to a different world. I did not see that life's portal was right in front of me for at least three years. This was not because I didn't want to enter a new life, but because I couldn't imagine how life could possibly feel good again.

Everyone around me told me that my loss would always hurt and I'd always be grieving. There was no more explaining after those ideas were uttered, no elaboration on how much grieving we were talking about. I read many memoirs written by people who had gone through a tragedy, and these authors placed so much emphasis on their losses that the idea of truly living life after loss, while in the midst of grieving, was never really addressed.

By the time I discovered the portal to a new world, I'd learned that when you experience a devastating loss from a death or a divorce, what you are left with afterward is a life beyond a regular life. It is beyond a day-to-day experience.

The day I accepted how different I had become because of my grief and realized I was no longer the person I used to be—and that I could never go back—a doorway opened. I stepped through it into a new life that had the potential to surpass my most ambitious dreams.

I was no longer someone who lived her life just like everyone else. I was no longer thinking in the same way as my friends, my family, and my co-workers. I was no longer

talking, acting, and feeling the same. So I stopped trying to fit into the life I had left behind. And I found that my pain lessened. My new self was no longer trying to match my old surroundings.

Trying to remake the old life was what had hurt me the most.

At first it was hard to make the transition to being a new me, as I had to practice laughing again and had to face my fears head-on by taking risks again. Above all else, I had to learn how to trust again. That was the feeling that took me the longest to recover. But once I did, it took me the furthest.

My reality today is almost too good to be true. A new man entered my life who understood my loss and the life I wanted after it, and we got married. As a result, we have four beautiful daughters together. I have a passion for my work that wakes me up every morning and excites me more than I ever thought possible. My new life is not a pale imitation of the old life. It's a vibrant, different life.

As I am writing this, part of me feels guilty for expressing the happiness that warms my heart. A little voice inside my head is telling me not to share too many details about my happiness, but I'm overriding it. Here is why I am telling you about my bliss: after my husband's death, I didn't think this life, this joy, this love, this fulfillment was possible.

I am here to let you know that no matter how old you are, where you are in the world, or how devastating your grief has been, you can shed your old identity and transform your life. How did I create a new life? First, I had to believe it was possible.

Now, it is your turn.

Chapter 2

THE SCIENCE
OF GETTING
PAST GRIEF

*The voice of grief is rather convincing, isn't it? It tells
you you're "too old," "not good enough," or "not worthy
enough" for another chance at life, that starting over is
impossible. This voice in your head is the first thing you
hear in the morning and the last thing you hear at night.
It drives with you to work. It stays with you at lunch.
Its message is so consistent that, because of its repetitive
power, you may be inclined to believe it. But, as persuasive
as the voice of grief is, everything it says is a lie.
It's all a pack of lies.
Do you want the truth? If you do, then start listening to
life calling to you inside your grief.
How? Every time you are yearning to be held and loved,
to laugh again, listen to your yearning. Do not listen to
your fear . . . Listen to life calling you: "I am here, come
on over. Take a chance on me. I am your life, and you're
all that I've got."*

You could say I was "courting" grief for years before we became intimate with each other. During college, I met and became casually acquainted with grief. I studied grief counseling, passed my exams with flying colors, and worked hard to practice my counseling skills at a local hospice. I was proud of myself, as I thought I'd made my dream of "helping people get through devastating pain" come true.

Back then, I believed I knew grief well.

But I was very wrong.

For the most part, grief and I were strangers.

It was terrifying, devastating, and ruthless, and it made no exceptions for me, the "friend" of grief.

As I was crying for myself, I was also crying for other people, because I realized that the help I had provided hadn't come close to what they'd needed. It had been based solely on theory, without the aid of real-life experience. Theory wasn't enough.

But the theory still held a fascination for me that I couldn't dismiss. There were many studies of the symptoms and the aftermath of grief. I felt that if I read these, I would learn something that would help me. But in the back of my head, I knew there was something else occupying my mind. I just kept thinking, *We know what grief does to us, but do we know what we can do to it?* This became the focus of my journey.

I tried visiting a social worker for grief counseling. I will never forget the lonely little chair I sat upon in that room. As kind and wonderful as my social worker was, my association with her produced few positive results. The woman had amazing listening and counseling skills, and she showed empathy toward me and my tragic situation. During my visits with her, I felt that my grief was being heard and acknowledged, and while this type of validation is a fundamental component in grief recovery, simply going over the story again and again did not help me heal. In fact, telling my story so many times made me feel so nauseous that I actually felt more grief on my way out of her office than on my way in. Our weekly meetings did not prepare me for life. Instead, they seemed designed to prepare me to live with my grief forever. I was a mess stepping outside into the cold wind, returning to the business of life.

Rather than trying to help me come back to life or rehabilitate me, this counselor and the world around me were simply working to help me survive this devastating crisis. That didn't seem like enough—for me or anyone. Just surviving, just scraping by, just keeping on keeping on didn't seem like the life I should be aiming for. How about loving again, laughing again, and living fully again?

Should I have been better prepared to grieve, considering that I had studied trauma and loss? Maybe. Realizing that I wasn't prepared was an eye-opener. The fact that I wasn't able to understand what was going on inside me and that I didn't know which way to go eventually prompted me to take a new look at my grief. When I did, I asked myself two questions:

1. What tools do I already have to guide myself through my pain?

2. What does science have to say about getting through grief?

These were the questions that I felt would lead me in a new direction. I wanted to find a way to do better for myself and for other people who were walking a mile in my shoes. So with that, the journey began.

The Beginning of the Discovery

I never expected that I would be interested in the mechanics of the brain. But once I started exploring it, I found myself eager to learn more. Brain science was hard at first, but it gave me so much hope for renewal and rebirth that I had to stick with it.

My first discovery happened in a truly simple way: one day, as I was browsing through the bookstore, I came across a shelf of books on the brain.

It was as simple as that.

Could these books help me understand what is going on while I am grieving? I wondered. I must admit some of the science was hard to piece together. Words and terms like *neuron, prefrontal cortex, limbic system,* and *basal ganglia* were unfamiliar. My brain felt about ready to explode from trying to understand them. Don't worry, I won't try to explain all these terms to you, because you don't need to fully understand *why* you can change your brain. I will focus more on *how* to do this.

I must admit the truth: much of the time, I had no idea what the authors were saying. For a while, my studies were just a hobby. I really had nothing to lose. Every other avenue I'd tried had led me nowhere.

My evenings were still tough to manage. I had no clue how to even begin to get to a better place emotionally until I came across a book called *The Mind and the Brain* by Jeffrey M. Schwartz, M.D., and Sharon Begley. Dr. Schwartz had made amazing advances in his work with patients suffering from obsessive-compulsive disorder

using techniques drawn from brain research.[1] I thought to myself: *Grief is obsessive and compulsive, too. You never know . . . perhaps this can lead to something.* As I read more, I could see that he believed we all have the power to shape our brains and our destiny. You can only imagine how my heart leapt at this news. I wanted to know all about it.

In reading Dr. Schwartz's book, I learned that the brain controls our reactions to the world—our emotions and our habits—by running certain programs based on our past. When we experience something, neurons in the brain make connections between one another, and these connections tell our mind and body how to react to the world around us. These connections are called neural pathways, or brain maps, and the more we use them, the more ingrained they get. And the more ingrained they get, the more likely we are to react in the same way. But our neural pathways can be changed so we can experience the world in new ways. We can create new habits and behaviors by working to consciously rewire our brains—by setting the right environment to push ourselves out of these well-worn neural pathways and onto a new landscape.

While Dr. Schwartz wasn't talking specifically about grief, this is how I related to the material. I saw that my brain was focusing on my grief, instead of on my life. Repetitive grief thoughts had created a map of grief inside my brain. Whenever I thought about my grief, I was reinforcing those neural pathways. In other words, I was contributing to my own suffering by making grief my default.

I also realized that if I focused my attention away from negative behaviors (like dwelling on thoughts about my loss) and toward positive behaviors (like learning a new skill or having a new experience), then I could actually change my own neural pathways. In other words, I could contribute to my own relief from suffering by breaking this habit of grief.

I became excited about the possibilities that this might hold, but I needed more information. I needed to see how to bring scientific theory into practical application, so I registered for a coaching program—Results Coaching Systems, developed by David Rock, Ph.D.—that focused on using insights from brain research to help people make changes and create the lives they want.

The more I learned in this program and the more I researched on my own, the more I realized that I could create a practical program to help people overcome their grief. I also realized that healing from grief isn't just about putting your life back together; it's about creating a new life that makes you happy. Through purposeful living, we can shape the brain in any way we like. We can even create a life that is more amazing than the one we were previously living. I know that it's hard even to fathom the idea of grief contributing to the fulfillment of our potential as human beings, but it's true.

As I created my program, I knew I had to keep the process simple and easy to follow, as grief had already made our lives so tough. I did not want to give my clients something harder than grief. I took the very basic foundation that the brain is malleable. I used the concept of creating new neural pathways and added a simple formula that gave control back to my clients and reminded them that they have the power to change their lives.

The Life Reentry Model, which anyone can follow, is a way of starting over after loss. It's a five-stage process

you can do on your own or in a group. It's important to know that you already have all of the tools you need within you to move past your grief and build a bright future. I know this is true because this process has been successful for me and for my clients, as well as for tens of thousands of other people who read my blog and online messages. This is a community of people that I call Life Starters.

What Happens When We Grieve?

There are three phases to healthy recovery after a loss. First, we exit our old life. Our loss forces us to leave behind the life we've been living. The normal routines of everyday life are disrupted. Some people believe that where we end up after that push-out of the old life is the next phase of life. But unfortunately, that's not true. In this confused and lonely state, we only end up in the space between two lives.

Second, we begin living in a gap between lives—the life we've left behind and the life we have yet to enter. I like to call this space the Waiting Room. When we're in the Waiting Room, we're still attached to the past—which is already gone forever—even as we're trying to figure out what the future looks like. In this place, we struggle with our new reality, thinking that it is our new life. We are unable to see ourselves clearly and make decisions as we used to. The brain's ability to plan and reason is temporarily gone.

Third, we begin to experiment with our new life. This is perhaps the scariest aspect of life after loss, because so much is unknown and has to be taken on faith. Little by little, we begin stepping out of the Waiting Room and entering a new reality. We start to do this early on, even though we haven't fully landed in the new life yet.

While these three phases address life after loss, the important thing to look at for recovery is what happens to the mind. The trauma of any event that slams the door shut on an aspect of the past—a divorce or a death—leaves its mark on the brain. We are left with uncertainty. We don't yet know what life will be like. We are afraid to take action and start over. Ultimately it is not the grief that stops us from starting life over, but fear of losing that life all over again.

Before we can really begin going through the process of Life Reentry, it is important to understand the relationship between fear and the brain. The *amygdalae*, which are almond-shaped masses of gray matter inside each cerebral hemisphere, help us process sensory input—to determine whether what we are experiencing is safe or dangerous. They do this by comparing what is happening in the moment to past experiences we've had. If an experience is deemed safe, we react in one way; if it is deemed dangerous, we react in a different way. When the amygdalae sense a threat, they trigger the secretion of stress hormones, such as adrenaline, which stimulate the fight-or-flight response, putting us fully on alert for danger.

Unfortunately, after a great loss, the world is uncertain and confusing. Everything seems like a threat because all you knew—that you were going to be with your love forever, that you were healthy, that you were safe—is now different. After loss, we perceive the entire world as dangerous because the amygdalae instantly compare new experiences with this trauma and what it meant in your life. This wears in the neural pathways of fear,

making the perception of danger easier for your brain, thus causing you to perceive danger where there isn't actually anything to fear.

Therapist Linda Graham, M.F.T., describes this phenomenon well: "The fast track of the amygdala relies entirely on implicit (unconscious) memories which, depending on earlier, past experiences, are more likely to be biased toward the negative and slant the meaning of an event toward a stress response, perceiving threat or danger where there may not be any."[2]

This unconscious habit of fear is what keeps people stuck in grief—stuck in the Waiting Room that is the second phase of life after loss.

While you wait in the Waiting Room, you get increasingly comfortable. This is your safe place. Some Waiting Rooms are actually quite cozy after we settle into them. Metaphorically speaking, if you can imagine it, they look like living rooms with nice, big couches and flat-screen TVs. You go to your Waiting Room initially to be safe while you adjust to your loss. But soon enough, your brain begins to associate stepping outside of this space as dangerous. We want to avoid pain, so the brain tries to anticipate bad situations before they happen. We stay in the Waiting Room for fear of risking future loss. Unfortunately, the longer you stay, the harder it is to start over.

Listen, all of us have to dance with our instincts to figure out when to leap and when to stay put. That's the challenge of being human and having a brain that evolved for survival. Having gone through a devastating loss, the brain feels threatened. It does not like to have its beliefs challenged, because it uses these beliefs to guard against threats to our safety. The life that we are looking at after loss challenges the beliefs that we had prior to the loss, so the brain does everything it knows how to do to fight against the emergence of the new life. Our survival instincts are so strong that we can be stuck for years.

We actually need to learn how to ignore perceived threats that come from stepping into the new life, and how to distinguish them from real threats.

How can you move out of the Waiting Room? By gradually learning to let go of your fear as you practice doing things that are different from your too-comfortable, self-protective routines. You have to learn to overcome your natural fear of change. This is the basis of my Life Reentry Model, and it allows you to take an active and strategic role in redefining your life after loss. It makes you able to create a launchpad from which you can create the life you desire.

Turning Your Loss into a Launchpad

The term *launchpad* wasn't part of my vocabulary when I was first grieving, and I never imagined that I would describe my healing process as launching, but that's what it ended up being.

After my husband died, I was in a very dark place, a place where there was no logical reflection on my journey, no understanding of my situation or where I was trying to go. My one moment of knowing that things must change occurred for me so unexpectedly that it felt like grief had literally yelled at me in an angry tone of voice. I must admit, I was caught by surprise, and I was taken aback by its impact.

It happened while I was reading a book.

I remember the moment clearly. I was reading novelist C. S. Lewis's book about mourning the loss of his

wife, *A Grief Observed*, which is an intensely emotional book. I put the book down and cried after coming upon the sentence, "No one ever told me that grief felt so like fear. I am not afraid, but the sensation is like being afraid. The same fluttering in the stomach, the same restlessness, the yawning. I keep on swallowing."[3] I was sobbing uncontrollably. I had realized that my grief over the loss of my husband was hurting too much for me to remain as I was. I had to move. I had to transform. I was either to start living again or to grieve forever. But I also realized that fear about what my life would be was interfering with the natural cycle of grief, which should have been mourning, healing, and then rebirth. My huge stumbling block wasn't that I was too sad to try again, but that I was too afraid to try again. In that moment of recognizing I was afraid, I was released to move forward.

I had been trying hard to convince myself that life was worth living—living *fully*—with a broken heart. Yet I could not make myself believe this was true, and my beliefs about what was possible for someone in my situation (single mom with no job and two young daughters) were stopping me from taking the small steps that would ultimately lead me to build the launchpad for my new life. What I didn't know back then was that mourning is an experience of sadness that takes place in the present moment: the *now*, if you will.

I had been confusing the emotions related to mourning with the *what if*s and the *why*s that are related to anticipation of the future. Because my brain wanted me to be safe, my head was being filled with negative beliefs about who I was, what I could accomplish, and how the world would respond to me. My thoughts were telling me that my present-moment grief would extend forward forever, and that I should therefore fear the future as an unpleasant, unhappy experience.

None of these ideas was real. This became obvious to me in a flash as I read that C. S. Lewis book and began to connect the dots between my thought patterns and my current state of being.

I had read about the malleability of the brain, so as soon as I saw that the thoughts I was having were not serving me, I knew I had to alter my thinking if I wanted to create a life that I'd love leading. I didn't know what that life would look like, but I did know I wanted to become happy again and for the unbearable pain I was feeling to quiet down. In the year since my husband had died, I had been miserable and sad most of the time, with very rare exceptions.

I realized that even in the midst of loss, I was in charge of my life. I saw that I still had the freedom to choose. Seizing hold of this insight, I began to make changes. But I knew that I needed to do this in a way that my fear-addled brain would be able to handle. I made small changes at first, such as painting the walls of my house a different color, replacing my car, and going on small road trips with my daughters. As small wins, or successes, took place, I began to feel confident again. My brain started to let go of its fear, which allowed me to risk a little more every day. My launchpad gradually built itself underneath my feet without me even realizing it.

Of course, all these special wins did not take place overnight. There were days in between that were very difficult to get through. But hope crept in more and more frequently, and launching out of the Waiting Room became more of a reality.

Being Strategic about Your Life

You'll never hear me suggest that you should be able to get over your grief and overcome your fear of starting over in a few weeks, 30 days, or even a few months. The pain you are going through is devastating, and it doesn't have a switch that you can turn on or off. It would be callous to give you that kind of simplistic advice. That being said, you do need to know at this juncture that you can live—even live *well*—while you grieve. It is possible to rebuild your life and love again, and faster than you might be imagining you can.

Launching a new life is a strategic, active process. It doesn't happen by accident. People who are taking care of their day-to-day lives after loss believe they are doing the right things, but many times they aren't. If they are operating in the default mode of the old self, they will continue to experience the pain of resistance. This pain should not be mistaken for grief. It's like trying to put on clothes you used to wear comfortably, which no longer fit you. This is merely a passive survival of grief. The difference between this and strategically launching a new life is that people in survival mode aim to keep busy to distract themselves from their pain, whereas with launching, they focus on movement toward a better life for themselves.

Through my own launch, and from watching the people I have coached transition into new lives using the Life Reentry Model, I've learned that when we are starting over after a significant loss, we pretty much need to renegotiate everything in our lives. We have to reconsider all facets of life, from what we do for a living, to where we live, to what we do for fun, to how we conduct ourselves in our relationships with friends, relatives, and even our children. Most people who successfully transition begin by going back to the basics and making small changes. As they take charge of their destiny and shift their focus to answering questions like "What might I create?" and "What is my new identity?" their pain drops away, and they begin to be excited by the freshness of their lives. Although the new life is not always dramatically different from the old life, how they feel about their prospects is.

The Risk of Stepping onto the Launchpad

In order to start over, you have to be willing to risk experiencing loss again. I wish I could take this risk away, but it is part of living life, a part of starting over. If you want to create a new life, you have to risk experiencing some tears, some fears, and some mistakes. Above all, you have to be adventurous despite your grief, if you want to find out who you truly are and what you are made of. Risk is the key to laughter and passion. The Life Reentry Model gives you a structure and techniques for creating acceptable risk. It helps manage the fear that tells us that we shouldn't do new things, that we should stay where we are. That fear warns us against doing anything out of character, but you need to learn to work against it. For me, fear told me that I was a single mother and that was how I should remain. But I fought fear. I decided to go out on a second first date, and when I was getting ready to go, I felt numb.

I went anyway.

Even three years after my loss, when I decided to let go of my corporate job and start my company, Second Firsts, I often felt out of my mind with grief and irrational fear.

But I did it anyway.

Those awkward and painful moments transformed me into the woman I am today. Without the tough moments of those second firsts, I could not have been reborn with a new identity or truly stepped back onto the stage of life.

The truth is that I'm still wrestling to raise the bar of my life, as I may always be. My fear of loss still speaks to me every day. Even so, I choose to be courageous.

Using courage to carry out every single second first I need to experience in order to move forward more confidently has been vital to my happiness and success in my current marriage, my career, and my role as a parent. I was willing to take these risks because I had found a voice of courage. And this is the voice I'd like to help you bring out and listen to. This voice lives within you—within your heart, your soul, and your brain.

When it comes to the raw fear that paralyzes the heart and could stop a person from taking action, what's important to know is that leaping regardless of fear is a choice you can make every day. Because of this, the part of you that is led by grief finally will surrender to your determination to live again and to experience joy. These experiences will give your brain another basis for comparison. It will no longer have just fear to compare things to. Your successes will give your brain proof that stepping out of the Waiting Room may not be all bad.

You can give birth to your wings while you are learning to fly. I saw this in my own life, and I've seen it in countless others.

My client Josh, a 49-year-old husband and dad, was a wonderful man who really wanted to build a launchpad for his life. He also wanted to live passionately and find his life's purpose. Even though he knew he wasn't happy, what kept him in his marriage was the fear that he would not be able to create a better relationship or a happier lifestyle outside it. That fear had been speaking to him for years. It was so powerful that it was able to trick him into remaining in the life he no longer wanted.

When he came to see me, Josh had not experienced the traditional loss of a person. His loss was more the loss of joy and love—of the life he wanted to be living. He was already in the Waiting Room, waiting for the right time to make a transition. He wanted a divorce, because he was no longer in love with his wife. They had let go of each other emotionally long before, without taking the step of making a real split. Part of Josh's problem was that he didn't know who he'd be if he decided to divorce his wife and move out of the home they had lived in together for 20 years.

As an experiment, I asked Josh to invent a series of small actions that would give his brain proof that a better life was possible. This experiment turned out well. Both his brain and his heart experienced a shift. While playing with elements of a new life, he experienced days of happiness, connection, and a quality of life that he hadn't believed were possible for him after so many years of boredom and low-grade misery. Very quickly, he was ready to fully step into a new life.

There was so much excitement in his voice when we spoke about the things he was doing, that I knew Josh had found exactly what he needed to climb onto his launchpad. The memory of taking those actions was now stored in his brain. It would always be there to remind him of an alternative to the life he was living. He, indeed, had his proof that another life was possible.

As time went by and Josh came back for additional sessions, he would talk with me about those exciting days of taking action and would reexperience the feelings he had when they took place. Ultimately, Josh did not choose to go for the divorce. Instead, he changed his career and started to build a new identity through his work activities. As he changed, his relationship with his wife was also transformed. She saw Josh taking new risks and was inspired to take some of her own. She changed. They eventually found their way back to each other.

Josh didn't cross the bridge from his old life to his new life by moving safely. There was some turbulence along the path he chose. He had to make a few leaps of faith. Nonetheless, he gradually gathered enough evidence for his mind to believe that the turbulence would ultimately lead him to the life he dreamed of and deserved to have. Josh was finally willing to risk the life he knew for the life that he could barely see ahead of him.

STUMBLING BLOCKS TO LIFE REENTRY

Our emotions and an unwillingness to feel discomfort play a huge part in helping or hindering the passage to a new life. For Josh, one of the biggest stumbling blocks he ran into was guilt. He felt a lot of guilt about the people he might hurt by going after what would make him happier. Please don't think that I would ever ask you to hurt others so the life of your dreams can become a reality. That's not what I'm advising. What I would suggest is that you focus on trying something new that feeds your soul. If you are in a place in your life where the larger purpose of your soul is no longer being served, and it is only grief or guilt that is holding you back, then you don't have a good enough reason to stay in this place.

The question you and I, and Josh and his wife, will always be facing is the same: *Are you willing to risk the possibility of more grief so you can find your way back to life?*

When I posed this theoretical question to my blog readers a few months ago, many people responded with comments like "No, I am not willing to risk pain for the chance to start over" and "I am afraid to walk out of my house, never mind trying anything else." In other words, they lacked trust.

Lacking trust is a huge reason that millions of people choose not to look for a launchpad. Many who have been through a loss believe they can never trust anyone again. They would prefer to be alone at home every night with their dogs or cats, watching the television set. Why are they unwilling to risk again? Because they believe that the future will be sad and painful.

I'm certain that those same people would be willing to face more risk if they knew what steps to take in order to launch a happy life despite the pain of the past.

Learning to trust that your life can change and be as good as or even better than it used to be is fundamental if you're going to have a chance at happiness. The first step to building your launchpad is finding the proof you need that the life you dream of is possible. This is what the Life Reentry Model can help you find.

Resolving the Conflict of the Launch

Grief walked into your heart and created room for your soul to grow. In that space, your soul has been, and is being, strengthened. I believe in the strength of your spirit. And I believe that loss can be a launchpad into a new dimension of living, loving, and thriving. If you've experienced a tragedy, your soul has traveled far, far away and into worlds that cannot be touched in any other way, by any other emotion. Grief opens your heart so you can undergo transformation. But it is up to you to take this expansion and spread it everywhere in your life. You must understand that while grief has opened up your heart, your brain will be telling you to hide and play it safe.

There are dual forces competing within you. One wants you to stay as you are; one wants you to evolve. You have to face the challenge of reconciling these forces. This reconciliation will be like a dance. Sometimes you'll be leading the dance, and other times you'll be following. Soon I'll show you some ways you can dance around your brain, breathe in life, and evolve your soul through the emotions that have drilled themselves deeply and indelibly into your heart.

Some of the exercises you'll be introduced to in the chapters that follow will be done through action and some through solitary reflection. Solitude is necessary for you to adapt to your loss. As psychiatrist Daniel J. Siegel, M.D., says in *The Developing Mind,* "Each of us needs periods in which our minds can focus inwardly. . . . Solitude is an essential experience for the mind to organize its own processes and create an internal state of resonance. In such a state, the self is able to alter its constraints by directly reducing the input from interactions with others."[4] Periods of reflection will slow down time, awaken you to notice what's happening around you, and help you to organize the data that you accumulate. Solitary reflection is especially necessary when our lives are destabilized following loss.

How our brains work is one of the evolutionary advantages of being human. As biologist John Medina says so well in his book *Brain Rules*, "The journey that brought us from the trees to the savannah gave us some structural elements shared by no other creature."[5] He continues, "There are two ways to beat the cruelty of the environment: You can become stronger or you can become smarter. We chose the latter. It seems most improbable that such a physically weak species could take over the planet not by adding muscles to our skeletons but by adding neurons to our brains."[6]

It is human to survive by adapting and evolving. Grieving is a natural part of how we evolve as individuals to respond to the challenges we face.

Stepping onto Your Launchpad

In working over the years with people who have experienced different types of losses, I've come across an interesting pattern. As they are proceeding through the five stages of the Life Reentry Model, it is quite obvious that they are releasing the tight controls they once had on their lives. As a result, many of them make major changes. The more shifting they do emotionally, the more their slight, nagging sense of *Maybe I need to change* begins to be felt as a deep, urgent need, rather than a choice.

I have witnessed major changes of lifestyle not only with the one-on-one clients in my private practice, but also among the people who post on my Facebook wall and send me comments after receiving my weekly newsletter, *Message in a Bottle*. Since I started teaching the five stages, I regularly receive announcements of new jobs, first dates, new relationships, engagements, and weddings—of second first steps being taken.

What can I say? Even though grief takes center stage when we go through a loss, as soon as we are able to sneak life back in, we can create miracles.

Right now, I could show you how the world after heartbreak and loss could be. I could go on and on about this whole new world of miracles. I could give you more words of hope.

But I won't.

I won't tell you what you can discover.

I won't tell you what can happen or what you can experience.

I won't do any of the above, because the magic of life after loss comes from the charm of the unexpected, the charm of falling in love again when you didn't know you could, the charm of catching someone smiling at you in the midst of a tough day, the charm of catching yourself laughing again despite having a tortured heart. It is the surprise of what a life after loss can offer you that makes it special.

Periodically you will get a sudden jolt of feeling lucky, a jolt of experiencing life through the lens of *hope.* Your good fortune can sneak up on you while you're just about to have another day that you believe will resemble the last 365 of them. We can't predict which day it will be when the magic of life after loss takes place.

You'll recognize it.

It is in the darkness of your heart that life shines a light. It is in the center of the storm that it throws in a peaceful moment. That is the only way you will believe that it's possible for life to turn around, face you, and smile at you again. It is the only way you'll be convinced that life can surprise you and catapult you to a brand-new beginning.

It's amazing, the way we can be catapulted toward life even in the midst of loss.

Loss creates an unbelievable amount of space for life to enter in. What you feel as emptiness is *life's new home,* and what you feel as loneliness is the urge to hold life's hand again.

Prepare to be surprised as you read about and participate in the five stages of the Life Reentry Model. Prepare to be surprised by the launchpad you build below your own feet. I wish for the emptiness in your heart to be filled with life's glorious ability to bring you joy when you least expect it.

Breathe joy, and then let's get started . . . over.

Chapter 3

LIFE REENTRY STAGE 1: GET REAL

There is a door within the space of your sadness.
You hold the key.
Open it.

When it comes to grief, it doesn't matter where you come from or what color your skin is.

It doesn't matter how old or young you are, how many lovers you did or didn't have, or how many or few mistakes you think you've made.

Grief is grief.

I don't care about your religion.

I don't care whether you have no money or you're affluent.

I don't care whether you are popular or not. I care that you wake up every morning and smile at the person you see in the mirror, even when grief tells you not to.

I care that you speak to yourself kindly, and do your best to give yourself hope when it feels like there's no hope left—especially when grief tells you to keep busy.

I care that you spend time with yourself, imagining a new life, dreaming of what could be. Regardless of how much you've lost or how many of your dreams were shattered, please remember to keep dreaming.

Above all else, I care that your heart keeps beating with life despite your loss—no matter your circumstances, net worth, or list of accomplishments.

Your heart doesn't care about the mistakes, the losses, the language you speak, or who your family is. All your heart wants to know is whether it can count on the next beat, the next pump of blood, the next breath. Right now you just want to feel a tiny bit more alive. You want to survive.

Surviving is necessary and good, but feeling as much pain as you do now is not.

Are you familiar with the feeling of helping someone who needs you?

Can you remember giving hope to someone else?

That's the same kind of compassion I ask you to give yourself.

Get Validated

Through my work with clients and having taken my own journey of grief, I've discovered that without validation and acknowledgment, we cannot heal. Our grieving hearts need us to receive validation for our pain. If we don't get it, we continually question our pain, our loss, and ourselves. We also continue to feel confused and uncertain about how things took place prior to, and during, the loss. The story of our grief stays alive.

As long as the story of our grief is alive, we search for acknowledgment for it everywhere we go, instead of

focusing on creating a future. If we meet someone new, we make sure to let him or her know what we've lost, and why we're different because of our grief. Our identity becomes wrapped around the new thoughts that grief has created in our minds.

On my Facebook page, "Second Firsts," which thousands of Life Starters visit every day, I often ask people to describe their losses and tell me who they are. Of all the posts I write, these get the most responses. Many people will write intimate details of what they've gone through and who they've lost in the comment box. Then the chain of comments goes on and on, because people are receiving validation that they haven't been able to get elsewhere. They are revealing a part of themselves that was hidden within them until they were invited to share.

It is important to us for someone to see what we see and remember, as this helps us gain more clarity about what happened in the past. It helps us understand why loss hurts as much as it does. It feels good to be seen, heard, and understood. Each of us deserves acknowledgment for our losses.

So let's start your process of validation right here, and right now.

Yes, you have gone through a devastating loss.

Yes, you have suffered tragedy.

Yes, you feel sad.

Yes, you feel angry.

I hear you. I recognize you.

I see you.

I see me in you.

And I know you see me in you.

Your loss was real and significant. It shattered you. It broke you down. It brought you to your knees. I know it did. I know you barely survived. But fortunately, you did. Your life has continued despite your loss and your trauma. This brings you to the present, right here, a moment when you can choose to validate yourself and take back a bit of control.

What do I mean when I say "validate yourself"? I mean acknowledge the truth of your pain. Let it speak its truth and listen to what it has to say. Listen to the patterns that emerge from your thoughts and discover what your beliefs are creating for you in your life. It may feel like you are cleaning out old closets that have been shut for years.

Having gone through my own loss, I'm eager to help you to better understand the experiences you're having. The surprising thing you most need to know at this stage in your grief is that many people continue actively grieving—sometimes for years on end—if they do not sufficiently acknowledge their losses. This confuses the brain, which wrestles with the contradiction between the experience of loss within themselves and the continuation of life outside, in the real world.

The way to resolve your contradictions is to get real with yourself about two things. First, get real about your feelings and beliefs. The rug of your old life was pulled out from under your feet, and you probably don't know where you stand anymore. Loss can create tremendous uncertainty because so much of how we define ourselves comes from our relationships and the social roles we play: wife/husband, mother/father, and so on. Your marriage is gone, and so you and your life are different. If you're feeling uncertain, then your confidence is likely to be shaky right now.

I understand that you may feel as if your life is out of control. Please know that this is to be expected after all you've been through. Having experienced a big loss, it's normal to be flooded by sorrowful emotions, pain, lethargy, and disorientation. The trauma of the loss and how it has disrupted the routines of your life is bound to generate confusion and bring up memories of past struggles, difficulties, and failures, including negative beliefs about your capabilities and worth. Recognizing all of these things is essential to validating your experience—seeing the full truth of what it has done to you.

Second, you need to get real about what your daily life is like right now, to take stock of your reality. Even if the reality is sad or ugly, it is the truth. You may be spending five hours a day crying. Your cupboards and your refrigerator may be empty because you haven't gone grocery shopping for a month. You may be refusing to pick up the phone and isolating yourself from your friends and family. Whatever the truth is, you can work with it. Going forward, the 360-degree snapshot of your life today will serve as a baseline against which you can measure your progress. You'll know you've made progress in starting over when you perhaps only cry for two hours a day and pick up the phone every third time it rings.

The best way to start getting real is by acknowledging your feelings and beliefs.

VALIDATING GEORGIA

The first time I recognized the power of self-validation to help people heal after their losses was when I was sitting across from Georgia, who had recently been divorced and was grieving. She had, in fact, experienced multiple losses in her life, including the loss of her innocence from childhood abuse and the loss of a brother who died in combat in the Iraq War. She was grieving these losses as well as feeling sad about the end of her marriage. Early one morning, I received a call from Georgia asking for an emergency session, as she had to tell me "something of great importance." I agreed to meet her.

When she walked into my office, Georgia was clearly anxious to speak to me about some unexpected events that had taken place. She hurriedly sat on my white leather chair, took off her coat and scarf, and placed them on the floor next to her. I sat down in the chair across from her, ready to listen and take notes on everything so that I could help her navigate her life after loss. But then, to my surprise, Georgia started talking about people I'd never heard of in previous sessions and describing incidents that had taken place years earlier. Without showing signs of any emotional difficulty whatsoever, she moved around these events as if in real time.

Five minutes into the session, I realized she was trying to cleanse herself of these experiences all at once, as they were getting in the way of her life. She'd suppressed them for so long that now we were unraveling her losses together; they were all coming out for air. It was as if these events themselves *wanted* to be heard. Sensing how important this process was, I allowed her to speak without interruption for almost an hour. Nearly out of breath, Georgia eventually stopped, at which point I asked, "How have you been able to live your life with all of these events weighing on you?"

She burst into tears and said, "It's been very difficult."

I asked, "Why do you think you've lived this way for so long?"

She answered, "Because nobody ever acknowledged my pain or loss."

"You came here to share news of something unexpected that happened yesterday. Have you even begun telling me about that yet?"

She said, "No."

We both reflected on that insight for a moment. Then I asked, "What would it be like if you validated your own life experience before seeking confirmation outside yourself?"

"I don't know."

"Well, given that you've spent the bulk of our session talking about the past, what's going to happen to this present concern? Who will take care of that now if not you?" This question stumped Georgia. For the first time, she became aware of how much her unconscious grief was costing her. It was interfering with her ability to live her present-day life.

At some point, Georgia had fallen into a passive mode of surviving her grief. Believing she needed to break this habit, I gave her an assignment to do before our next meeting. I asked her to do a Grief Cleanse: to write about her pain in a journal in order to make space in her mind so that she could think about issues that mattered to her in the present. My hope was that she'd use this as an opportunity to reconnect with herself and reflect on what she cared about. She needed to do this before she could make any kind of decisions about her future.

Validating her own grief was a much-needed first step in Georgia's reentry to life. It was so powerful, in fact, that by our next session, she was ready to make important decisions.

Like Georgia, most people discover that they can validate themselves. Others also discover that there's a specific person, such as a parent, spouse, or sibling, whose acknowledgment they are hungry to receive. Knowing this makes it possible to ask for acknowledgment and move forward—even if they don't actually get the validation they hope for. Knowing what they need gives them options.

What can I say? If you've suffered a traumatic loss and want to avoid being entranced by grief for the rest of your life, you're going to need to get present with your grief at some point and let it speak its truth to you. Grief that hasn't been allowed to have its say will continue to interrupt your thoughts and dictate your behavior. A good way to listen is with the Grief Cleanse.

The Grief Cleanse

The Grief Cleanse is a technique for validating grief that makes it possible to release pain you've been holding on to. This transformative exercise does require a bit of concentrated time, but when you're done with it, I promise you'll be able to begin moving forward in your life.

To prepare, go to your local stationery store and buy a large blank notebook. If you'd rather type than handwrite, set up a document on your computer, giving it a name that's easy for you to remember. For example, you could call this document "The Pattern of My Grief."

Open your calendar or schedule book and block out a 30-minute time slot every day for a whole week. Consider these appointments *sacred*. This week is the period you're

allotting to give your grief the urgent attention it wants, so that you can take back your life.

Here are the guidelines for your seven Grief Cleanse sessions.

- Find a place where you can sit comfortably and be undisturbed. Then, to begin, take some deep, slow breaths in and out. As you do so, do your best to release the tension in your body.

- Next ask the question, "Grief, will you come out and speak to me?"

- Notice whether you experience any resistance to this question. On a scale of one to ten, with one being extremely uncomfortable and ten being very comfortable, note your level of resistance to letting your grief free. Make note of the level in your journal.

- Remove any resistance you feel by reminding yourself of the reason why you need to do this exercise. This "why" could be your children, your happiness, your future, or another specific reason that is meaningful to you. Repeat this step until you reach a feeling of comfort when asking the question, "Grief, will you come out and speak to me?"

- Once you've removed your resistance, ask the question again. This time around, since you are not feeling resistance, you will have room to think and feel other things. Make note of the first feeling or thought that arises. Has grief been dying to come out and speak to you, or is it reluctant?

- Write in a stream of consciousness for the remaining half hour, documenting everything grief wants to say. Simply let your hand write as your mind speaks, without censorship.

- Are you becoming aware of any surprises in what grief is telling you? Write these down. Also observe words that keep repeating themselves. Look for the patterns of emotions. Write these words down in a separate part of your notebook.

- Observe your body while you are writing. Is there any tightness or stiffness? If yes, stretch and relieve the discomfort. You may be allowing your grief to be expressed, but the aim is to do so with your body intact. Sometimes physical pain is connected to the surfacing of suppressed emotions.

- Once your 30-minute cleanse is almost done, pause to consider what your feelings are. Capture them on paper before you move on to the rest of your day or evening. Remember to be aware of the new feelings that are arising rather than the old pattern of grief. See these thoughts as the ones that will be able to shape your future life.

- Now that you have acknowledged the reality of your grief, your final question should be, "What is the one thing today that I most wish other people (or a specific person) would acknowledge about my loss?" Write down your answer. Remember, you don't need to ask for acknowledgment from others yet. Before making a request like that, you must understand the exact thing you need acknowledged. See if for now you can give yourself acknowledgment for the new feelings and thoughts that are emerging.

Many people avoid reflecting upon their grief because they fear feeling pain. What they don't realize is that a good portion of the pain they feel is actually the pain of their resistance to grief. When they do this exercise for several days in a row, they report that the pain lessens and they start to feel relief. I've even heard people say it feels good—pleasurable—to experience the grief.

I'm recommending this process because it's important for you to take charge of your grieving. By ensuring that your loss is fully experienced and properly acknowledged, you'll make room for yourself mentally—space in which you can slowly begin to imagine a time after loss.

THE INFINITE LOOP OF LOSS

Neuroscience tells us that the period after a loss is when we are at our least comfortable and most vulnerable.

The loss of our old identity leaves us confused and frightened about the future. The fear centers of the brain are activated. So even though we need to have clarity to make good choices, the brain tries to prevent us from thinking about what is happening to us now. As science writer David DiSalvo explains in *What Makes Your Brain Happy and Why You Should Do the Opposite*, this is one of the shortcuts the brain wants to take that usually doesn't lead us where we should go.[1]

Instead of reflecting on our present circumstances and the decisions that will lead us to a better future, the grieving brain attempts to master the loss by preoccupying itself with the past. As human beings, we carry our personal histories with us, etched in our brains. The past, present, and future are commingled. Problems begin to arise if the sadness we feel that originally started out as mourning a loss becomes a ritual pattern of reliving painful thoughts and memories.

Have you noticed that the place you keep visiting in your mind does not change? That the story you are reliving follows the same script, with the same ending? I call this place, this script, the *infinite loop of loss*. It's like being on a roller-coaster ride that carries you around and around without ever letting you off. The last ride is always just as painful as the first. This is why it's so important to break the cycle of grief.

In doing your Grief Cleanse, you gained your first introduction to something I call the Watcher, a calm and very wise part of you that is able to observe your thoughts objectively—without the emotion attached to them. You consciously chose to put some space between your pain and your life. You chose to look at your life not through the eyes of grief. Those who are able to watch

their thoughts and feelings, and name them, feel they have more control over their lives. By activating your Watcher, you established some distance between you and your pain; you learned to detach emotionally from the pain and discover ways to heal. Being able to do this means that you are no longer letting your loss and your pain define you.

In his book *Mindsight,* Daniel J. Siegel, M.D., describes the capacity of the Watcher as a "kind of focused attention that allows us to see the internal workings of our own minds. It helps us to be aware of our mental processes without being swept away by them."[2] Being able to develop mindsight in the midst of your grief is essential to your present and future emotional health. You need clarity so you can take stock of where you are in your life at this moment, as opposed to where you imagine you are. It is important to experience the reality of life without the intense presence of your grief casting a shadow over the world around you. Even if your loss took place recently, you may realize, by watching, that you do still have occasional moments of authentic joy. You are likely to discover a lot of surprising information by activating your Watcher and letting this part of you explore your thoughts and feelings.

At first, you may simply gain a glimpse of the capacity of your Watcher. Later on, your ability to stand back and observe will be stronger, and you'll be able to bring it out at any point. This will help in your quest to stop the infinite loop of loss in its tracks, and thus you will prevent yourself from strengthening the neural pathways of grief in your mind.

Right now, the distance between you and your thoughts and feelings of loss may be so slight that your grief colors everything in your world. After doing the Grief Cleanse for seven days, you will be familiar with your Watcher. My clients and the participants in my Life Reentry program have described feeling greater clarity after the Grief Cleanse, and this clarity grows the more they learn to activate their Watcher. When it comes to the decisions and steps we need to take in our lives after loss, clarity is essential.

Activating Your Watcher

You'll need a pen and paper for this exercise. When you're ready, go to a comfortable place where you can sit alone for a while without being interrupted, to reflect on six questions. Spend several minutes writing about your answers, using the writing prompts that are provided.

If this exercise seems too difficult to do on your own, for any reason, you may recruit a friend to help you through it by asking you the questions and listening to your answers.

There are no right or wrong answers. There is only what is true for you.

Question 1: When you wake up in the morning, what is the very first thought that comes to mind, and how does this thought make you feel?

Answer/prompt: "I feel . . ."

Question 2: Where in your body is the feeling you are describing located?

Answer/prompt: "This feeling is located in my . . ."

Question 3: Is there a feeling you would like to experience instead?

Answer/prompt: "I would like to feel . . ."

Question 4: When you experience this new feeling, what would you like to have in your life?

Answer/prompt: "I would like to have . . ."

Question 5: When you acknowledge what you would like to have, do feelings of unworthiness arise? If yes, where do they come from?

Answer/prompt: "My feeling of unworthiness is coming from . . ."

Question 6: Most likely, your feelings of unworthiness are not warranted. Why do you deserve the thing you have identified?

Answer/prompt: "The truth is, I deserve this . . . because . . ."

Doing this exercise on a regular basis can help you establish the habit of bringing out your Watcher. It will reinforce the neural pathways that help you see the world and your feelings objectively. This will begin the shift away from grief.

GETTING REAL WITH JULIE

Julie joined my Life Reentry program after her husband left her for a younger woman. I remember the first time I heard her voice over the conference line as she shared her story of loss with the group. She sounded anxious. Julie told us that she'd met her husband, Joe, in high school. She got pregnant shortly after graduation and they married. She became a stay-at-home mother, taking care of their daughter and household. Joe worked at a local gas station. All seemed well with their family for many years, and Julie was very happy with her husband.

Julie then described how one day, without any warning, she came home from running errands and found a note from Joe on the dining room table; it said he wanted a divorce and was never coming back. Julie began crying as she revealed how ashamed she felt and how scared she was now to start over. At this point, I gently interrupted her.

Interrupting someone who is in a lot of pain is one of the hardest things to do, because I don't want to seem rude. In this case, I felt Julie had transported herself to the past. I wanted her to come back to the present, where she could use her ability to reflect on her thoughts, her Watcher, to get some much-needed clarity about her situation.

I asked Julie to tell the group what one feeling she most often felt as she was waking up in the morning. She said, "Dread." I then asked her where in her body she felt this feeling. She seemed surprised that I'd asked, but knew exactly where the feeling was located. She said, "In my chest."

Then I asked her what kind of thoughts made her feel a sense of dread, and she said, "Thinking about what my neighbors and friends must have said when they found out Joe only left me a note on the table." She said she also felt shame when she thought about their comments.

"Were you surprised by your thoughts and feelings as you were telling us this story?" I asked.

"I'm surprised that I didn't mention missing Joe or wanting him back," she said. "Since he left, I've been trying to find a way to get him back. But the way he did what he did was terrible. No wonder I've been so sad. My real goal is to wake up in the morning and feel happy."

As Julie discovered by reflecting on her feelings, although we often believe we want one thing, in reality we want something entirely different. Getting clear is what the Watcher can do for us. And being able to activate that Watcher when you need it is very important in stopping the loop of loss.

If, right now, you're spending a lot of your time caught up in the infinite loop of loss, it may be because you're protective of your history and do not want to let it go. This is understandable. But please also know that in riding this ride, you're not really showing yourself compassion or self-love. Though it's okay to grieve, it is not okay to keep replaying the same mental tapes that trigger negative feelings and beliefs. For as Deepak Chopra, M.D., and Rudolph E. Tanzi, Ph.D., so astutely observe in *Super Brain*, "Your brain is always eavesdropping on your thoughts. As it listens, it learns. If you teach it about limitation, your brain will become limited."[3]

Fortunately for you, you can learn to look at your past in a brand-new way just by daring to step outside of your repetitive thoughts of grief. By thinking new thoughts and engaging in new activities and learning, you can exit the loop of loss.

What you need to know is that we don't lose our memories by living well after loss. On the day we accept that we've changed, a portal opens to a new life that has the potential to surpass our most ambitious dreams, or even to fulfill dreams we abandoned at some point in the past.

The moment you realize how different you now are from the way you were before your loss, I promise that you will stop trying to fit into the life you left behind or stay there in your mental time travel. Then you'll grow quickly forward from the present into the future.

The past doesn't leave.

Message in a Bottle

Your grief is not here to end your life and destroy your soul, but to bring you back to life. Your grief is not here to punish you, but to teach you how to live. It's here to set you free.

Grief is actually sitting next to your life. The two of them are close friends who are talking about you and all the other grieving people in the world. Life complains that it doesn't get as much attention as grief, and grief says: "Be patient, dear, they will come to you when they are ready to leap to higher ground, when they feel they can let go of me and trust you again. When they were with you, they got hurt, so do you really expect them just to bounce back and come running to you?"

Life then turns around to grief, stands up, and with a smile says, "My dear grief, do you know who you are talking to? I am life. I am the essence of the world. I am medicine for the sick and air for the lungs of the brokenhearted souls. If they knew life was right here waiting for them, they would never turn away from me."

So I am here to ask you this question: If you knew your life was sitting right there next to your grief, wouldn't you grab it by the hand and go live it once again?

With Life,
Christina

GET A 360-DEGREE VIEW OF YOUR LIFE AFTER LOSS

You may think and truly believe that, after being pushed out of your old life, where you've ended up today is your new life. Unfortunately, if you're like most people, this isn't true. Many people remain in the Waiting Room. Even though it's obvious that they can't go back and pick up from where they were, they don't really say good-bye and close the door behind them. Thus, they remain chained to the past.

If your exit from the old life hasn't been done mindfully yet, you need to reflect on what is now different about your life and behavior, and absorb the reality of your loss.

Previously I asked you to do two exercises to help you get real about your thoughts and emotions. Now I want you to set your emotions aside and get real about your behavior.

Pull out your journal again and go find a quiet, comfortable place to hang out undisturbed for about a half hour. When you're situated there, answer the following questions.

- What did you used to do that you are no longer doing?

- What are you doing now that you didn't do before?

- When was the last time you laughed?

- When was the last time you cried?

- When was the last time you went out on a date?

- When was the last time you phoned or saw a friend?

- When was the last time you told a joke?

- When was the last time you went to your favorite place?

- How long ago was the last time you felt truly alive and enjoyed a moment in your life—and what was happening on that occasion?

- What have you done so far to start your life over? (List the actions you've taken.)

- What is different about you and the people around you? (Be specific.)

- Are you still trying to live the life you used to have?

- Which part of you has been locked up since your loss?

- Which part of you has been in charge since your loss?

- Have you challenged yourself lately?

- Have you been following the same routine every day since your loss?

How much of your time do you spend thinking about your life before your loss? Right now, it's important for you to become aware of the way you're living your life. In the days ahead, things will change. Perhaps these questions will stimulate you to make new choices. At the end of this exercise it's important to ask yourself the following questions:

- What surprised you the most from the answers you gave to the questions in this exercise?

- Did you discover something about your life that you were unaware of?

Getting real about your life after loss is just the beginning of a long-term transformation. I invite you to do the same exercise a month from now and see if anything has changed. See if being aware of where you are today actually has allowed you to make changes. The answers to these questions should guide your journey forward.

THERE IS A NEW LIFE WAITING FOR YOU

Grief is a factor in the evolution of our souls. It takes us to heights of self-knowledge that are not possible without the experience of loss, especially when we start to remove the fog of our grief through our relationship with the Watcher and through asking ourselves the tough questions of the 360-degree exercise. All it takes to reach these heights is to catch a glimpse of the light that shines through the impossible pain that a divorce or a death brings. Once we are able to see life through the grief and through the truth of our present reality, hope takes over. Like jump-starting an engine, the power of hope and clarity can create a jolt in our lives that quickly gains momentum. A spark of hope in the midst of grief can be used to create any new beginning that we can imagine and believe in. In a hopeful moment, we can learn that it's possible to get off our knees, stand up, and learn to walk and talk again.

I know it may be hard to believe right now, but grief can open the door to an amazing new life. You can start over again, no matter how devastating an experience you've gone through.

Having felt grief, you'll discover that your heart is able to feel gratitude for even the simplest happy moments. Your soul now possesses the wisdom to understand the depth of what those moments mean to you. I promise, if you'll only open the door to believe that life is yours for the taking, life will lead you on a journey that would never have been possible before. All you have to do is get real with yourself and start activating the Watcher within you so you can tell yourself the truth about your life after loss. Asking the right questions, activating the Watcher, and really looking into your life by discovering what you have and what you want is a great start in this journey of reentry. Remember that the infinite loop of loss will want to keep looping, and it is your responsibility to keep asking the questions and validating yourself in the process. The very important thing to remember is to stay present and aware by speaking to your grief when it needs acknowledgment and by having the Watcher help you find the truth.

Message in a Bottle

I used to lie to myself. My list of lies got quite long, especially when I was grieving. It was so big that it felt like I was adding at least *two new lies* every day.

I lied about everything, even about going to the grocery store, cleaning the house, going out on a date, not being present with my girls, hating my job . . . and the list went on. But the *biggest lie* I would tell myself

was that I was *a victim of my circumstances*. The more lies I accumulated, the more passive I became toward life.

One day, by accident, I started telling myself small truths. Things like:

- "Maybe I can go on a road trip with my girls. It can't be that hard."

- "Okay, maybe one date—he might not be the worst guy in the world."

- "I should apply for that job. You never know, I might get it."

Then it started happening. Small miracles would come into my day. I got the job, the date was good, the road trip rocked, the grocery store was not too far to get to after all.

I learned that I had to stop the lying and start living in my truth. It was hard at first. But when I did, life showed up with a big smile on her face.

I know it is not going to be easy for you at first. In fact, telling the truth will be hard in the beginning. It's harder to tell yourself the truth than to lie and do nothing.

Hold on tight. Prepare yourself for the storm.

Get ready to fight for your life.

Get ready for the most important battle: the battle to be honest with yourself, the battle to walk out of your comfort zone. Opening the door to the truth is never going to come naturally. You may actually have to force your hand.

I am going to ask you for something very important. It is this: Don't overthink the truth, analyze it, mull it over, or talk about it with everyone you know. *Just be honest.*

When you start to see yourself through the eyes of your own truth, you will become the rebel that you have always been. The warrior you know you are. The lover you promised you could be. The doer and the fighter.

The fighter for the truth.

Now, I am not saying you might not tell yourself a *white lie here and there*. Just don't grow the list like I did. The list

of lies is a trap that holds you away from your dreams, that keeps you inside the loop.

Go write down your list of lies. Then draw a vertical line down the center of the page and add the list of your truths across from them.

You know which list I would go with.

With truth and some dare,
Christina

Chapter 4

LIFE REENTRY STAGE 2: PLUG IN

When everything looks the same on the outside, yet everything has changed on the inside, we break. We break in half.
This is the duality of loss.

Starting over can be tough at first because we feel so afraid and have so many doubts about the new life that is ahead of us. When we lose someone we've become attached to, it is disorienting and terribly uncomfortable. At such a time, the brain interprets anything new and unpredictable as a threat to our very survival. It will accept only the slightest discomfort before a full-blown fight-or-flight response is triggered.

You know what that's like. At even a hint of danger, your heart beats faster, your breathing gets shallow, and your digestive system shuts down. It's stressful. Unfortunately, after a terrible loss, fear may be screaming at you all day long to go into hiding. I call this voice of fear your Survivor. It yells at you in an effort to protect you. To keep you safe from the world. Your daily life is so full of panic that it tells you to build a fortress around yourself and install heavy locks on the gates. Aren't you ready yet to stop listening to your Survivor and leave your Waiting Room and step into the life that awaits you? I understand that you probably don't even want to try.

Or if you do want to try to leave the Waiting Room—even temporarily, as an experiment—I'm sure you wish it were possible to begin to live, laugh, and love again without feeling as much doubt, remorse, anxiety, and confusion as you do.

I hear you.

But hang in there—help is on the way.

In Stage 2, you're going to learn a way to replace fear-induced procrastination with action, confusion with clarity, and waiting with moving on. I'll teach you about the *plug-in,* a simple yet powerful technique with which you may connect to your new life just a little bit at a time, so that you won't feel overwhelmed or too scared to function as you do so. In fact, you just might find it fun.

The 5 Percent of a New Life

Loss can be catastrophic to your life, to your soul, and to your identity. Nonetheless, it was an event that took place at a specific point in time. The time you are living in now is not *that* time. To begin to leave your Waiting Room, you will need to plug in to the present-day life around you as much as you can—perhaps only by as much as 5 percent at first. As the intensity of your grief subsides and you become stronger, you'll plug in to life in greater percentages.

When I speak about 5 percent, I am asking for just a little bit of your attention, energy, and time; you want to

nudge yourself toward reaching the outcome you desire. I mean 5 percent of your attention, 5 percent of your energy, 5 percent of your time, and perhaps more important, 5 percent of the potential of the outcome you want to see. For instance, your desire may be to remarry, but dating scares you. A 5 percent plug-in for the dating scene might be spending an hour seated in a coffee shop reading a book, or you could sign up for an account on a dating website. Five percent is a low-risk, low-effort action that helps your brain realize you are safe.

You need to begin to pump positive bubbles of life into the space of your grief on a daily basis if you ultimately want to do more than just survive your loss. Beginning to live, laugh, and love again is essential for your future happiness—for the full-blown, *extraordinary* happiness that you deserve. I therefore encourage you to begin taking small actions right away to participate in the world. Those actions are plug-ins. They will help build new neural pathways.

Plug-ins are not about "faking it" until you make it. Rather they are occasions of dipping your toe in the water of life until you are ready to jump back into the river and swim.

Keep in mind that it's natural to want to dismiss the return journey from the world of grief. It goes against what we're being told by the environment around us, which is that we are injured and need to stop, hide, and rest until the pain goes away.

Even when we try to plug in to life with just a few small steps, we can easily become frustrated and angry about this unwanted transition from old life to new. When life is overtaken by grief, everything we do feels harder, slower, and more painful than normal.

The brain is telling us to be afraid. It says, *"What if I get hurt again?"*

The heart isn't ready to love again, or to let go of the pain of the loss. It says, *"I don't want to love anyone else."*

Grief says, *"The situation is hopeless."*

But the situation isn't hopeless. It's just hard.

Sometimes plug-ins work immediately; sometimes they don't. Sometimes they lead to a deeper world of hurt that you have been hiding. Sometimes they open your eyes to opportunities that you've never seen before. The important thing is that they help you to reconnect with life, to step out of your grief for just a moment. So start small. Just 5 percent.

The Way Out of the Waiting Room

When you first start to plug in to your new life, it will feel like being in a 3-D movie theater. With each plug-in you do, you'll give yourself a very small taste of something you've never had before, or that you haven't had for a while. You may sob uncontrollably after laughing for the first time in a long time. You may be in shock if you notice your heart beating faster again when you meet someone new. Your palms might sweat as if you were a teenager, and you may wish you were back under your cozy blanket at home when this takes place. You see, the taste of life after loss—however good it feels—can also be uncomfortable.

This is to be expected. After all, the unknown is feared even by people who are living without the prior experience of loss, so imagine what it's like for us when we've been conditioned by loss to believe that all we

have can suddenly be gone. Plugging in to a new life, habit by habit, routine by routine, we are slowly and surely able to change the old habitual pathways in the brain. We create new neural pathways, or *baby maps,* that strengthen our connection to the new life we wish to enter after we heal. The habits of grief are strong, though not insurmountable.

The longer we have been grieving a loss, the harder it is to start living again. This is one of the reasons why I wholeheartedly believe we must invite life and grief to walk hand in hand. If life doesn't escort grief back to joy, then it takes us much longer to get there, if we ever do.

Today, I invite you to begin opening the door of your Waiting Room by using the plug-in process. Take my hand, and let's unlock that door together. Turn the key left. Grab the door handle and push down. Take a step. And then another.

Easy does it—take it one step at a time.

When you try to initiate life bubbles in the midst of grieving, obstacles may appear in the form of doubts like, *Is it okay to go for a drive in the middle of the day, rather than lying in bed and crying?* Doubts may scream at you all day long if you dare to stretch yourself even incrementally past the point where you feel comfortable. Remember to activate your Watcher if you have to at this point. Fortunately, this is where plug-ins can do you some real good. As your doubts arise and you feel the physical discomfort of the fight-or-flight response, they can help to make doubts and physical symptoms manageable. Five-percent plug-ins are simple, effective tools that can start you on your journey back to living life more fully.

To do five minutes of exercise or one fun thing every day is absolutely fine if that's all you can manage right now. Since you know that your brain is malleable, you can understand that this will build maps in your brain that will make it easier for you to do ten minutes of exercise, for example, or two fun things, at some point in the very near future.

You're planting seeds of life whenever you do your plug-ins. As the intensity of your grief subsides, or you feel naturally pulled to participate more in the life of the world around you, you can increase the amount of plugging in that you're doing as much as you choose.

YOUR FIRST PLUG-IN

Where should you begin? The following three-part process will give you an idea.

1. Looking at your life as it is right now,
    what one thing is causing you the most
    frustration? (This could be a relationship,
    your job, or even something in your home.)

2. What could you do to resolve this problem
    or achieve this desire? (Be prepared for
    resistance in the form of fear to come up
    when you think about doing it.)

3. What is the smallest step that you could
    take now—one that would not make you
    too scared—to move toward resolution of
    this problem or achievement of this goal?
    (It should be an action so small that if you

failed on this step, you would be able to go
back to your comfort zone immediately.)

When you've identified the tiny step that feels safe
enough to do, you've found your first plug-in. It's a 5-
percent action. Write down the ultimate goal in your
notebook, and then go and take action on it. Make sure
what you select is small, realistic, and doable.

Even if it seems daunting right now, spending 5 percent of your day experiencing life in ways that are com-
pelling to you is the minimal amount of time you should
consider spending. Connecting with life again is a prior-
ity in order to counterbalance the negative reactions you
have to your loss with joy and other positive emotions.

This step in the Life Reentry Model is designed to set
up situations that are opportunities for you to exit your
brain's default setting of fear. Although these opportunities
won't change the way you feel about your loss, they will
gradually help you cope with the flood of thoughts and
emotions that arise in your mind as a result of grieving.

A plug-in can be as simple as taking a new route
to work.

Please don't laugh at the simplicity of the next idea,
which is to move the furniture in your home around or
paint the walls a new color. You'd be surprised at what a
difference this makes.

Try cutting your hair short or dyeing it a new color.

Get into your car and drive somewhere you've never
gone before.

Any of these actions could lead you to do further
plug-ins. It doesn't matter what you do exactly, so long as
it is different (at least in some small way) from anything

you've ever done before. Making change that is under your own control is a win for you as a survivor of a loss. Life has made the biggest change. Now you are responding and adapting. As long as you exercise some control over the outcome of the changes in your life, including those that are the inevitable consequence of grief's fury, you will eventually be able to get back on your feet.

Lauren's Very First Plug-in

In my Reentry to Life program, I work with groups of people who've been in the Waiting Room for a while. At first they are timid, quiet, and unaware of the nature of their behavior. My initial job is to help them see that their current life is not the one they will ultimately be living. It is not as great as the life they could live. It's the Waiting Room.

Though they don't have this clarity before the program begins, they soon develop it. Group work is incredibly powerful because when people can perceive the Waiting Rooms of the other group members, they finally start to recognize their own.

Lauren, a woman in her early 50s, participated in Reentry to Life. Having lost her husband three years earlier, she was keenly aware of the impact of grief on her life. She knew she was still transitioning from her old life to her new life, and she had a relationship with her fear. Even so, she couldn't get herself to take a single action that would bring her out of hiding. Lauren felt disappointed with herself because she wasn't able to take even the simplest of steps. She was no longer the woman she used to be, nor was she the woman whom she could become.

During one of the group calls, Lauren spoke to us about her fear and the frozen state she had found herself in. She told us that she craved interaction and communication with other people, but was afraid to put herself out there so this could take place. Her problem was that in her mind, she would imagine people's reactions to her, thinking these would be poor, and she didn't want to put herself into an uncomfortable position of possible rejection.

I asked her for the proof of the anticipated future rejection, and she said she didn't have any. She just expected it to be this way. In other words, she was guessing. She was inside the infinite loop of loss.

Lauren's loss had been sudden and traumatic. As a result, her brain interpreted the world as a threatening place—one to be avoided. It told her, *"If you go out and socialize, people will reject you."* Once she recognized that this particular belief was her mind's default setting, she committed to doing a first plug-in. She accepted an invitation she'd previously turned down to go to a friend's birthday party.

On the next group call, a week later, Lauren reported she had gone to not just one social gathering, but three! Her actual experience of socializing at the birthday party had been so unlike the fear-based projection she'd formulated that the experience transformed her thinking. With that, she'd started to trust the process of plugging in to life and believing that taking one small step at a time would allow her to begin to lead a new and happier life.

As the weeks of the program went on, Lauren reported that she was plugging in socially on a regular basis. She also started looking for a new job. Being freed of her isolation felt so good that she realized that she desired a career in a social setting, such as a position in the hospitality industry. The first plug-in weeks earlier had allowed her to reenter her life with an identity that behaved differently than her fear had been dictating she behave.

My Early Plug-ins

The most difficult plug-ins I ever did after my husband died involved dating and romance. Meeting someone who might one day become as significant to me as my husband had been, and even starting over by going out on a first date, seemed close to impossible back then. Several months after my loss, I remember going out on a first date for dinner with a man in a nearby community, and my heart wanted to leap out of my body. Before I left the house, guilt started screaming at me so loudly that I felt sick to my stomach. I literally had to sit down and think through the decision again.

Fear was whispering to me, *"It is way too soon. You should not be so selfish."*

Doubts nagged at me: *You have little kids to think about, so what are you doing getting all dressed up and going out on a date? How dare you think of your own happiness right now?*

Nauseated and with heart palpitations, I got up and started getting ready. Fear followed me around the house, telling me, *"Just go to bed and watch a movie tonight. You need your rest because tomorrow will be another tough day."* I shut the door on that voice.

As I was responding to my inner voice of doubt, I saw myself trying to emerge from the fear that I had become so used to living with.

In those days, I felt as if the whole world had an opinion about when it would be too early or too late to be seen with another man by my side. For this reason, I remember going out on that date and not telling anyone about it. It was part of my secret mission to get *me* back. I knew I wanted and needed to get myself out of the thrall of the grief, shame, and guilt that had been surrounding me every day. By taking the risk of going out for a couple of hours on a date, I got to walk into the new life I had started to build.

In retrospect, this was a clever approach. Although that date did not bring me a soul mate, or even someone to go out with regularly, it did give me the courage to step out of the Waiting Room and activate my Watcher. I have to admit, it was not easy to pick what to wear for that dinner date, as the prettier I thought I looked, the louder the voice of shame yelled at me. I was ashamed that I was abandoning my husband and that I had the desire to be loved and shown affection. That day, I put in my emotional earplugs and stepped out into the world.

What I am here to ask you is this: when will you take your chance to go on a secret mission, wearing earplugs that protect you from your own inner critic if you need to?

If your plug-in is a date, remember, first dates don't have to be perfect. They only have to be right for you for where you are today, not for where you will be a year from now. Mr. or Ms. Right needs only to be right for right now.

There is one more thing you need to know. The right person for you right now is someone who may like you more than you like him or her. This individual really has to think the world of you, because every time he or she looks at you, it is like holding a mirror up for you to gaze into. What your date sees, you see. It's important at the beginning of your journey back to life that you build your confidence by getting your feet wet, not by trying to find a partner for the rest of your life.

Yes, you read that right. The purpose of dating after a divorce, death, or breakup is not to find someone to fall in love with immediately. The purpose is to feel loved, liked, and simply adored. You are rebuilding your identity and reconnecting with your interests and desires.

My initial frightening plug-in ultimately brought me to a second first love, my husband, Eric, over a year later. Going on that first date, and other similar dates, gradually made me ready to meet him. After dating unsuccessfully for about a year and a half without falling in love or even being close to feeling much of anything, one Monday evening something happened that took me by surprise.

I used to take my girls to a support group for kids who had lost a parent at a place called the Children's Room. We would go there every two weeks for about an hour and a half. These evenings were good because my girls got to connect with their peers and share their feelings, which needed to come out, but were also hard to express because they were so intense. The parents would sit in our own support circle while our kids were sitting in theirs.

This particular evening, as I was sitting on the same chair I had sat upon all the other times I'd been with the group, someone new walked into the room and sat down beside me—a man about my age. Okay, I'm going to admit that I thought he was attractive. My heart started beating faster for the very first time since I couldn't even remember when.

This man was Eric.

The moment is as clear to me as if it were yesterday. When he looked at me and said, "It's really nice to meet you," I tried to act cool and collected. As I mumbled something in return, I thought, *Oh, wow, I'm nervous.* Then I started to count the days until the next group meeting when I could see him again. I remember telling my girlfriends about the cute new guy who'd joined the group.

Three months went by without my exchanging anything more than a few hellos and good-byes with Eric while we were arriving and leaving the support group sessions. Then, one evening after my daughters and I got home from the group, I decided to take a small, but definitely brave, action to get to know him better.

What I'm going to tell you next, I've never admitted to him until now, because I suspected he might tease me mercilessly about it, but I want to share it with you. I wrote an e-mail to the entire support group, asking if we could arrange a group dinner and an evening out. I was secretly hoping that Eric would say yes and come out with the group so I could get to know him a little bit more. This was the way I felt most comfortable connecting with him.

Can you guess who responded to my e-mail within a few seconds? Eric. He said he would be more than happy to go out with the group.

That night we e-mailed back and forth with each other a few times, and this ended up in us arranging a one-on-one date to go to the movies that weekend.

If we count the group e-mail as my first plug-in with Eric, you could say our first date together was my second. Going on a date with him was absolutely nerve-wracking for me since I really liked him. For three months, we'd been meeting in a group setting, and now we were about to go to dinner and a movie together. What would happen? Would it be wonderful?

I had no appetite for the two days prior to our date. So many butterflies were in my stomach! Then date night came, and we had a really great time together. We laughed and talked and got along well. At the end of the night, Eric asked me for a second date, and I said yes.

Second dates, in my opinion, are much harder than first dates. Whereas first dates mostly involve talking and maybe holding hands (we didn't even do that), on second dates, the thought of a kiss definitely comes to mind. I had been with my husband for ten years and on my own for close to two. I was truly scared out of my mind at the thought of kissing Eric. But I knew that life was waiting for me once again, and this second date with Eric meant the world to me.

We kissed.

I could not fall asleep that night. I felt like a teenager.

Was I falling in love?

This was something I'd thought could never be possible again.

That's how a simple plug-in can open the door to a new love.

FINDING WAYS TO PLUG IN TO YOUR NEW LIFE

I've already asked you to do one simple plug-in, but to really get the benefit of plugging in, you need to make it a bigger part of your life. So carry a notebook with you in your handbag or in your car. Whenever you have an insight about something you'd like to do in your new life, write it down in the notebook as soon as you can. You're going to use these spontaneous ideas to generate a series of plug-ins to do in the weeks and months ahead. If you're actively grieving, perhaps you'll only do one or two plug-ins a day. Stretch yourself to do more plug-ins when you're ready, being mindful of your limits. Your notebook full of ideas will be there when you're ready to challenge yourself.

Take a few days off from doing plug-ins if you ever need to. The process of starting over has to feel right all the way through. There is no reason to rush. It has to feel as if you were meant to be in this place. If it doesn't feel good, you'll need to revisit it later when you feel more ready.

As you do your plug-ins, write down how you feel about them. Embrace your guilt as well as your enthusiasm. Surprise is good, but you'll also want to embrace the upcoming changes in your life by writing down the steps you take leading up to them. Remembering the steps that took you through your transformation will allow you to gain a bird's-eye view of the change that has manifested itself after you've come through it. Later on, you'll see how important this is.

Your plug-ins are like puzzle pieces of the new life that is coming into focus. Some of these pieces will be physical, others emotional, mental, and spiritual. Some plug-ins will involve you in activities you never would have dreamed of doing before your loss. Some could involve reclaiming activities you formerly enjoyed and gave up years ago. Because of your loss, you now have an opportunity to investigate life as an entirely new person.

Making small-scale decisions, like joining a support group and going to the movies with an old friend, is vital right now because you're trying to discover who you are becoming. This new identity is not the same as the one you had before the big event of your loss disrupted your life. Such decisions are intended to be short-lived—meaning, they should lead to only brief experiences. Thus, they shouldn't be overly considered actions. At this point, having even a tiny glimpse of a possible new life is sufficient.

When you notice that you've undergone a positive shift from trying a particular plug-in, stay with that type of plug-in. Repetition is how the brain builds more complex and sustainable neural networks. The brain's ability to adapt to the environment and learn new skills will ultimately lead you to a new way of living and feeling.

As human beings, it's common for us to perceive our surroundings in an automatic way. When we've gone through a loss, grief takes control of these automatic perceptions. It tells us how to interpret what we see, hear, and otherwise sense. If we haven't examined how we truly feel about who we are, and what we should and shouldn't be doing, we need to do novel things that turn

off the brain's automatic-piloting system. That's what the plug-in does.

Explore the following ideas and their associated plug-ins at your convenience. These are some of the areas that I've seen help many people. Some look at your thought patterns, and some look at your interactions with the external world. Let these suggestions inspire you when you're creating your own plug-ins.

The Life of Your Beliefs

You have the power to change your life in a spectacular way simply by changing your thought patterns. To do so, you need only see where your attention currently is and then redirect it. If you send your mind conflicting messages it won't know which direction to turn. But give your mind clear instructions to go after what you want, and you increase the likelihood of success.

The best way to control your thoughts is to control your words. Words create a pattern of belief within the brain that each of us goes over, again and again, every single day. For instance, how often do you use words such as *angry, overwhelmed, sad, unlucky,* or *failure* to describe yourself? And when you do, how does it make you feel?

Begin to keep track of the words you use to describe yourself and your feelings about them. Stop using the ones that cause you pain.

To explore how you're using words currently, get out your notebook and a pen. Write one paragraph about your life as if you were describing it to someone you've only just met. Make a list of at least five adjectives to describe your life: for example, *adventurous, sad, happy, noteworthy,* or even *tiring.*

Then, write down the phrases you most often use to describe yourself in your conversations with your children and with friends; for example, "I feel overwhelmed with pain" or "I am so lonely" or even "I had a fun day today."

Next, describe how friends and family members choose to communicate with you. Do they ask how your day is in an empathetic tone of voice, or do they generally avoid the topic of loss? Would you say that their words are uplifting and positive, or disheartening? Overall, would you describe your family as having a positive or a negative influence on you?

Finally, what is the number one topic you think about every day? If your thoughts tend to reinforce your perception of yourself as a victim of circumstances, unlucky, stuck in a rut, or grief stricken, would you be willing to do some plug-ins to turn that perception around?

Examining the input your brain is receiving on a regular basis might be a startling exercise, but it's a very important one, because it will wake you up to the nature of the words that you have been using to define yourself. No matter what you just learned, it's always good to feed your brain some positive input. Practice choosing your words wisely, and also do a Belief Plug-in.

The Belief Plug-in: Create a positive affirmation that fits your life interruption perfectly. For example: "My divorce has made me stronger" or "I am open and incredibly focused on finding peace, love, and comfort in my life again." Three times a day, stand in front of a mirror, look into your own eyes, and say your affirmation seven

times in a row with passion, conviction, and happiness, so that your brain can start to rewire itself. Try saying:

- "My grief has made me unstoppable, and I am now able to take more risks to create the life that I want."
- "During my post-loss life, I've learned valuable lessons that I now use every day to create a phenomenal life for myself."
- "I am unbelievably blessed to have another shot at life."
- "I am smart and happy and someone who can be focused on my goals."
- "I feel good when I'm with my family."
- "I am determined to create the life of my dreams."

The Life of Your Home

When my husband died, I changed the colors of the walls, I moved the furniture around, and I shifted the energy of the house by adding different elements to it. I wanted to bring my house into the present moment. I did not want to walk into my house every day and be reminded of what had just happened. I wanted this house to have a new personality, a new way of expressing itself, a new identity that matched my new way of looking at life. My perspective was shifting, and it was resisting the physical reality of my home. I needed to match what was happening within me with my immediate external world.

The very first time I did a live call with hundreds of people, I asked them to look around and see if the room they were in looked like their life in the past or their life in the present. Most people shared that the room they were in looked so much like the life they used to have, it was almost like time had stopped. I was surprised that this simple exercise made so many people so much more aware of their surroundings. Plugging in to your house and bringing in change by shifting the physical environment you live in will allow for new thoughts and new experiences to come in. Your brain will begin to look at your life from the present moment and not from the past. It is important for our immediate environment to start looking like the new life we are creating.

In this exercise, you're going to go from room to room through your house, starting in your bedroom, and explore your feelings and the memories associated with each room. Bring your notebook along so you can document your discoveries. We first want to get real with the physical space before we begin changing it. We want to know the feelings each room brings up. Once we become aware of them, we will ask ourselves what we need to change so the desired feeling will be part of our daily existence in this room. For example, when I came back from the hospital after my husband died, I walked into the bedroom and I knew I could not sleep if the bed was facing the same direction as it always had. So I asked my parents to help me to move it. I moved it to the other side of the bedroom, and I slept that way for months. This plug-in helped me shift to the present moment.

So let's begin the home exploration.

The process goes like this. Seat yourself comfortably, take a few deep breaths, and begin observing the room as if you were visiting it for the first time. Just look around and take it in. As you scan the room, what is the first thing you notice that you haven't noticed before? Describe your thoughts and feelings in your notebook.

Repeat this process in the bathroom, in the kitchen, and in your living room.

Then think about your house in general—not room by room—and answer the following questions:

- In your home, do you live in the present or in the past? For example, is the house full of photos of the person who is no longer with you?

- Is it a place where you see yourself living in the future? If the answer is no, what are the plug-ins you need to act on so you can initiate the selling of your home?

- Do you feel better when you are outside of the house or when you're at home? If the answer is that you feel better outside, then this plug-in exercise is very important for you. Creating a space you enjoy inhabiting is a fundamental part of your healing.

Once you answer these questions, you will begin to feel that there are many decisions to make. You will also start to feel overwhelmed, as I am sure there are many things you want to change. But before you reach the state of feeling overwhelmed, tell yourself that all you are about to do is choose one room to change. You are going to start bringing in new life to your house one room at a time. By walking around your house and observing it as if you are visiting for the first time, you allow your Watcher to tell you what is necessary to turn your home into a safe haven.

The Home Plug-in: Choose one room in your house to change. Whether you paint the walls and rearrange the furniture by yourself or bring in a professional interior designer to help you doesn't matter. What matters is to have a space in your home that breathes life back into you and allows you to step out of the comfort zone of grief so that you can begin to enter your new life. Once you plug in to one room and are enjoying your time there, start the process over and plug in to another room in the house. Before you know it, your home will start to resemble your brand-new life, the life you want to create after loss. You will spend a lot of time healing in there, and your physical environment will influence your thinking. Remember, we want to keep out of the infinite loop of loss. Watch out for thoughts that tell you that you do not have the time to update your home, or that you do not have the money to do it. This is your brain trying to keep you in the Waiting Room. Plug in to your house and reenter one room at a time.

The Life of Your Friendships

If someone had told me that most of the friends who were with me during the year of my loss would not be in my life in the future, I would not have believed them. I would actually have laughed and walked away. I was very protective of these friends, because they stood by me during the hardest period of my life. But as time

has passed, I have seen my relationships with some of them change. Some have become stronger; some have gone away. For those I've stopped spending time with, it is not because they no longer are good people. It's not because of any clear conflict or fight. It is just that I changed so much internally that what used to connect us was no longer there. This is part of creating a new life, and I would like to ask you to be okay with that. It is important that you allow yourself to let go of relationships that no longer work for you. Of course some of the relationships might be stronger than before, so you must be open to this change as well. The truth is that the reality of your relationships as they were before your loss, and as they are afterward, is not the same reality at all.

After a profound loss, it's important to figure out which relationships to renegotiate, which ones to end, and which ones to keep intact and start plugging in to more often. The questions in this exercise will help you make some decisions. By getting real about what you need from your current relationships, you will start bringing more people into your life who resemble the person you are becoming. In doing so, you will be plugging life into your emerging identity. I am going to ask you to be a little selfish with this exercise and to really commit to creating a safe haven around you. I can assure you that guilt will send you some not-so-truthful thoughts about your friends—watch out for those as you start to ask the questions. Guilt will try not to rock the boat or go through more loss. But what is important in your life at this stage is to slowly open the door for more of the people you want to have along for this journey of reentry. If you agree with me, then let's begin.

- How many friends do you speak to on a daily basis?

- How many new friendships have you developed since the loss?

- Do you initiate calls with your friends, or do you wait to hear from them?

- Are you open to invitations?

- Do your current friendships fulfill you?

- Do you feel as if you need to explain yourself over and over again?

- Do you feel lonelier when you're around your friends?

The Letting Go of Friendship Plug-in: Which relationships in your life create a downward spiral of emotional energy? Find a relationship that brings you a lot of discomfort and negativity. Once you determine which this is, take the first step to let go. What is that first plug-in? For some people, the first plug-in would be to journal about ending the relationship. In this way, you would be bringing in the Watcher to clarify your thoughts. Journal about all the things you like and don't like about this relationship. Share with yourself how it would impact your life if you let that relationship go. Why would it be important to do this right now? If you conclude that you want to move forward with letting the relationship go, then you must do this in your own way and at your own pace, in a manner that is comfortable to you. If writing an e-mail to that person is the way to go, then do just that. If not answering the phone serves you better, then please let that call go. This plug-in is not about being

polite or politically correct, it is about taking care of you. It is time, don't you think?

The Feel-Good Friendship Plug-in: There are some people who have been a big part of our lives and history. They sometimes know us better than we know ourselves. These friends are part of our DNA and life story. But even though we know who these people are and how good they are to us, grief can remove them from our routine. I am here to remind you that these folks are part of the healing process. You need their listening ear, their warm hugs, and their honesty and help. The Feel-Good Relationship Plug-in is about learning to receive these friendships during these tough times. So let me help you bring these friends closer during this difficult time.

Which relationships from your life before loss feel strong and make you happy? Pinpoint the friends you feel good around, and reach out to them with a phone call or an e-mail. Remember to plug in to these important relationships in 5-percent increments, as you're able. They are part of your history, as well as of the new life that you want to bring forth. Be sure to make the effort to say yes to their dinner invitations and their efforts to bring you outside the Waiting Room. I know it is not easy to be social when you are feeling grief, but doing this in small increments will help you tremendously. For example, say yes to only one dinner invitation a week. Be in control of the door that opens toward your new life. You have the keys in your back pocket—always remember that—and if you are having a tough day and you have said yes to dinner but don't feel like it, just be honest with your feel-good friends. You know they will understand.

The friendship plug-ins keep you honest and truthful to your desires. Without owning the truth, we will not be able to reenter life in the manner we so deserve.

The Life of Dating and Romance

Sooner or later, most people who experience trauma figure out that keeping busy lessens the pain. Keeping busy feels like running around in the brain's labyrinth being chased by grief and being able to stay one step ahead of it. You know grief can catch up when you stop and think, or when you stop and feel—then grief takes over, and you are its captive.

After my husband died, my life's protagonists were my two daughters and me. I did not see or speak to anyone else during the week. I went to work full-time in the corporate world, knowing I had to focus on proving myself as a professional. But I was also a mother who absolutely would not rely on her family or babysitters to raise her kids, so my daily schedule was kept full from working and raising two kids under the age of seven. That helped me manage my repetitive grief thoughts, but it was also tiring and overwhelming to keep busy around the clock.

You would have laughed out loud if you could have peeked inside my head and my heart when dating was added to my "the busier you are, the less grief you feel" list. I was trying so hard to move on in my life, yet it felt like I was tied to a big bull that was pulling me in the opposite direction from romance. For every one step forward in action, I took several backward in emotion. In retrospect, I can see that I was lying to myself about

my readiness to move on. On every date, a thousand truths came knocking on my door to reveal how much I missed my husband. With each date, my grief was subsequently reactivated.

Trying to make your heart feel something when you are grieving is like trying to drive a car without gas. You keep turning the key, and nothing happens.

I'm sure you have heard the saying, "Don't make any decisions in the first year after your loss." My version of that advice is this: Make the decision to start living, and be open to what happens when you open the door to your new life. Also be open to what is *not* happening, and stop doing things if they're not working out. It's okay if you're going on a date because you are afraid to be alone, or just to numb the pain. Stop judging yourself and be present with your needs in the moment. You might be going out to have fun or to find a soul mate, or both! Please leave your guilt at home and step outside your front door with life by your side.

So let's find out what it is that you want when it comes to romance after loss. Write your answers to the following questions in your notebook. It is important to capture these answers because they will help you get real with where you stand today.

- What is the paramount belief that you have about finding love again? Does your brain tell you that it is going to be hard or easy?

- If someone you had met only once asked you out on a date, what would be your impulsive response?

- Are you willing to experiment by going out with someone completely different from the person you are no longer with?

The answers to these questions come from the way that your brain is currently wired, but to bring in a new life, you really need to look at them. If your paramount belief serves your life after loss—not your life prior to your loss—this is great.

The goal here is to realize where you are now so you can start to react more consciously to romantic situations that may come up, to pause and think about your response. For example, if you are deciding against having a relationship with someone because you are genuinely not attracted to them, then that is absolutely right. But if you are saying no to this relationship because you assume that it won't feel right because of your past experiences, then you are again stepping into the automatic settings within your brain.

The Romance Plug-in: It's time to do one small plug-in that will lead to the possibility of dating—if not a date itself. If online dating seems like it would be the best place to meet potential companions, do a little research to find out which dating site suits your personality— then sign up for it. If dating in a social environment captivates your imagination, make sure you attend one small-scale social event in the next few days. Taking action reinforces your connection to life. But remember to answer the questions before you do your romance plug-in.

Make Fear Your Best Friend

At some point, after you begin doing plug-ins, fear is going to jump out of the shadows and tell you, *"You're not ready to start again."* Even with just 5 percent invested, you are not immune to the effects that fear can have on you. In my own life, fear tried to stop me more times than I can count. I had multiple conversations with my fear until one day I decided to look at it for what it really is—a worried friend. It was trying to protect me. To keep me safe. To prevent pain. And when I started thinking about it in this way, I realized that instead of arguing with fear about the actions I was taking, I could make it my best friend and reassure it that everything was going to be okay. So I wrote a letter.

> Dear Fear,
>
> I know you're here to protect me because you want to keep me safe.
>
> I know you worry about me because of all that has happened in my life.
>
> I know you can't help yourself, which is why you immediately come to my side whenever I take a new step.
>
> It's going to be okay. I'm only going to take one small step today. So there's really nothing to worry about.
>
> I'll keep my keys in my pocket and come home safely tonight. During my travels, I will love myself fully. I'll care for my body and soul. I just need to learn to walk again.

And, Fear . . . I need to make you my friend. I know there are no scary monsters on the other side of you. I know you are just trying to protect my heart from being hurt by all the hardships of life.

Love,
Christina

Now, my dear Life Starter, I invite you to write your own letter to your fear. Once you have written the letter, put it somewhere you can see it and read it every day to encourage yourself to take a few small, deliberate steps outside of the safety of your house and plug back in to life.

Message in a Bottle

The truth about starting over is that it doesn't just happen on its own.

Your next chapter in life, your second firsts, won't just show up at your door with a big smile.

The truth is: It's all on *you.*

Even though I believe in my work of Life Reentry, as I have been able to help many people mend their broken hearts, it was not because of me that they healed. It was because of the actions and work they did during the weeks we spent together.

It was because they did not stop when everything seemed to be going against them.

Because they believed in the life ahead.

They wanted to start over.

They valued life more than they valued grief.

They allowed themselves to laugh again, love again, and act again.

It was not because I am amazing and profound. Let me say this loud and clear: *The credit belongs to them. Not me.*

I so wish I had the ability to heal everyone. But I don't. Without your help, I cannot help you.

You are the one who wakes up every morning and looks at yourself in the mirror and has to find the strength to smile back. You are the one who feels the heartbreak in your chest and chooses to breathe through it.

You are the brave one to ask for help.

You are the one in the arena fighting for a chance at a second first.

Without you and the courage you demonstrate, I cannot help you.

What I am about to ask of you today is to give yourself some tough love. I am going to ask you to step outside of your routine this weekend.

You see, grief lives in a timeless way. It meets us in our past, present, and future. It greets us in our reality and in our thoughts, in our sleep and during our waking hours. Grief knows very well how to fool us into believing that our hearts are still very broken, incapable of healing.

The only way we can break away from grief's chambers is by taking action outside of the routines of grief.

Just know that it will be uncomfortable at first to feel fully alive again. *It will not feel good to get out of the Waiting Room.* Your brain will lie to you as much as possible, giving you many reasons why you should stick to your schedule.

Am I asking for a lot?

With responsibility and action,
Christina

Chapter 5

LIFE REENTRY
STAGE 3: SHIFT

When the dream that was no longer can be, you have to dream a different dream.

You know that voice in your head that's very quiet, like a faint whisper?

The voice you ignore on the days you'd rather not step into your power?

This is the voice that holds a clue about your divinity, your power, and your human capacity to create something, even after falling so far down that you are certain no one can find you to help you back up. This voice speaks to the self that has been touched by grief and says that it has also been touched by life and that you have more of value to contribute and experience.

When you refuse to listen to this voice, you shut down the life force within you.

When I heard the voice of my life force calling to me during my period of heavy grieving, it required me to step into my divinity and create something magnificent. It required me to push myself out of my comfort zone, let go of my wounded self, and find my inner dreamer.

When I stepped out of my grief and experienced my early second firsts, I underwent a process of self-discovery. My Survivor was competing with the new positive thoughts I started to have. I had to learn how to shift from my Survivor thoughts to the thoughts that were coming from living once again. At first I must admit it was not easy; I had been very comfortable in my discomfort. But I knew I had to consciously train my brain to gravitate toward thoughts that stemmed from the new life I was creating for myself. Finding a way to shift your attention away from the negative voice of fear and toward the positive voice of the dreamer is a necessary step for anyone who is starting over. You need to get your brain ready to reenter life.

Don't be fooled. The person you temporarily become after your loss is not the real you. The identity that's created while grieving is based upon pain, fear, guilt, anger, sadness, and a broken heart. There is a different identity waiting to be revealed. A real evolution takes place in the brain during the days, months, or years following a loss—and it holds exciting possibilities. It can lead to an extraordinarily happy, productive, and fulfilling new life. The purpose of Stage 3 in the Life Reentry Model is to facilitate the positive evolution of your brain and your thinking.

In this chapter, I will show you how to make a mental shift from the life you left behind to the one that is waiting for you. You started this process in the first two stages by getting real with your life and creating ways to plug back in to the world around you, but now is the time when you're really going to consciously work on shifting your thought processes to look to the future. The shift you make will come in two phases: exploration and affirmation. I will guide you in using the Watcher to look at your current life to discover the negative beliefs that are sabotaging your choices. Then I will help you figure out what you would like to be different—what future you would like to work toward. Once you have this picture, you will be able to shift your beliefs. Once this exploration has occurred, I will show you three ways to reinforce the changes that you have made and to show your brain that these shifts in attitude are good and safe. In the process, you will be introducing new beliefs to your mind, and your eyes will be opened to a wider field of options.

The goal is to end the habit of repeating thoughts of loss by instead repeating thoughts of life. Without making this very slight frequency change within your brain and your heart, living the full life you so richly deserve after loss won't be possible.

Remember, if your loss was recent and your grief is fresh, it's important to mourn the loss. It's important not to resist authentic grieving. But distinguish between true mourning and the repetition of loss. Repetition of loss is a natural, albeit ultimately unhealthy, practice of going over the *whys*, the *hows*, and the *if onlys* of your past long after a loss has occurred.

Happiness Is a Choice

It took me a while to understand a simple truth about loss and healing: Happiness lives inside of us. It is not dictated by circumstances. Even though I'd seen thousands of grieving people have internal experiences of healing, my own loss gave me a very different perspective. I had to go through my own full cycle of loss and recovery before I could discover the truth.

This discovery that happiness is a choice we must repeatedly make, day in and day out, rather than an event-based experience, set me free from my attachment to loss and enabled me to shift my focus toward living my life. Once I saw this truth, I chose to become happy again.

When we go through a huge heartbreak, we're likely to hold on to that loss with all our hearts and souls, and base all our unhappiness on the details of that loss for a while. It's easy to confuse unhappiness over the loss of someone we loved with sadness over the current state of our lives. Even if a loss took place years before, we tend to still talk of it in the present tense, as if it is affecting us right now—because it is. Memories connected to strong emotions have an immediacy that's incredibly powerful. Unfortunately, because of its magnitude, loss shadows reality in such a way that we can miss seeing all sorts of other reasons for why we aren't happy.

We can fail to recognize that one specific loss—as important as it was—isn't, and couldn't be, responsible for all of our unhappiness. Many things contribute to our level of happiness.

One of the biggest factors I've seen that keeps people from choosing happiness is their inability to detach from their former self. Detaching from loss can only truly happen when you're able to shift your identity enough that if, in the future, you were to meet the person you lost—or even meet yourself!—you would have to get reacquainted, or reintroduce yourself, as the case may be. The further away we move from being the person we were when the loss occurred, the less pain we experience.

This type of shift of identity can only happen when the brain is experiencing new habits and routines.

A true, sustainable shift into a new life is not just the feeling that follows an "aha" moment, or when we say yes to taking a particular action once or twice. It's the continuous momentum of an action-oriented life, the nature of which is the byproduct of developing new neural pathways.

As you continue doing your plug-ins, you'll experience a series of tiny, temporary shifts into your new life and then retreat again. These new thoughts and actions will eventually bring forth a new identity, one that represents the next evolution of you as someone who both underwent a severe loss in the past, yet has been having experiences in the present ever since. Being a fixed personality is an illusion. Your evolution won't ever stop.

Your task at this stage of starting over is to practice shifting your identity permanently from a persona of grief to a persona of life. Remember, you have to choose happiness, part of which is about detaching from your grief. You also need to become aware of your personal power to navigate your feelings of grief. You may not understand yet how powerful you are . . . but you are, and you'll sense it very soon. You are now becoming a warrior of life, shifting your focus to a perspective that contains life as its primary ingredient. As a warrior of life, you'll be someone who knows how to endure, fall down, get up, have experiences, and learn through commingled tears and laughter.

It's likely that one day soon you'll cry with joy when you recognize how you are changing and begin to experience new feelings, new relationships, and a full-blown new life.

Maria's Shift

Maria was one of the very first Life Starters I coached. She walked into my office with the biggest smile I'd ever seen and shook my hand. My first impression was that she was smart and energetic. As we spoke together that day, however, I realized she was lost in a world of low self-esteem where she couldn't see her own light or access her brilliance. She admitted that at one point, during the first few months after her husband died six months earlier, she'd neglected herself so much that she wasn't even brushing her teeth in the morning.

The woman in front of me couldn't see herself the way I saw her, as someone extraordinary. She was the mother of two amazing kids she loved a lot, but she'd lost touch with her identity after being a stay-at-home mom for seven years. She'd always defined herself as a wife and mom. Even with the hefty life insurance payment she got when her husband died, she would soon be forced to go back to work. She wanted to find work that inspired her, but before she could do anything else, she had to pull herself together. She was lost in a sea of self-neglect.

"How long has it been since the last time you did something for yourself?" I asked her.

"Almost a year and a half," she said, and then burst into tears. "That's when I got a gift certificate for a massage for my birthday from my husband." She missed him tremendously.

Though Maria wore sweatpants and no makeup, and only had her hair swept into a simple bun, she was beautiful. As the session wore on, after the tears, her smile would always return. It was obvious to me that she was a warrior, a woman who could come back to life easily,

and I wanted to help her access the courage she needed to improve her life after loss.

"I know you've probably asked yourself this before, but bear with me just a little, because I have an important question for you to consider," I said. "That is, if you could wake up tomorrow morning and be the woman you were born to be, who would you be?"

Tears began falling on Maria's cheekbones as she heard me ask this. My question had opened up a huge stream of emotion. Without any hesitation, she answered, "I would design kids' books and be a successful book designer." As soon as she spoke, she put her hand over her mouth. We both gasped. It was as if she didn't know where those words had come from. As she was speaking them aloud, something magical took place. There was a sparkle of life in her eye. To me, that was a sign that she had made a very important internal shift. During the rest of our session, we went on to talk about what the future would look like if she pursued this idea.

Do you wonder what it was that shifted her? What put the sparkle back into her eyes? My belief is that inviting the possibility of being a book designer into our conversation gave it some validity, which was enough to trigger a shift in her brain that allowed her new self to emerge.

The shift Maria made from focusing on grief to focusing on life was so powerful for her that after that single session, she started to take better care of herself. She went on to do numerous plug-ins. She made changes both inside her home and within herself that improved her life. She became much happier. Over four months, she lost 35 pounds of excess weight. She also started working part-time and going to design school, hiring a babysitter in the afternoons to watch the kids while she focused on her studies. Although she didn't become a children's book designer immediately, she soon made a plan of action and began taking steps toward her big dream of designing professionally. Hers was a sustainable shift of identity.

You see, the woman with the sparkle in her eyes who loved designing had been right there from the beginning of our interactions, just waiting to come out and be acknowledged. On some level, Maria was already waiting for the conversation. She wanted a chance to look at her prospects, so that a shift would take place from the old self to the new. After six months of grieving, she had put herself in a situation where this inner shift toward life could be felt strongly. Though it happened in my office while talking with me, it actually could have happened anywhere that Maria's new self was given room, opportunity, and the invitation to emerge. If you do not have a professional to ask you this question, choose a good friend to come over for a cup of coffee or tea and ask her to gently bring this question up within the conversation you are having.

This is truly a great start toward a sustainable shift of identity. Once you see the glimpse of a new self emerging, hold on to it by adding the plug-ins that will help you bring more of that identity into your life. Most of the time, doubts and negative thoughts will try and hide that first glimpse of the new you. This happened to Maria quite often. So let's find out how we can reverse the fears that will try to stop you from experiencing those amazing second firsts.

REVERSING YOUR FEAR AND MOVING TOWARD LIFE

To make a shift like Maria did, you first have to come to terms with where you are today. As you've learned, the human brain can serve as a magnet for negative thoughts, which then inspire negative behavior. Put in simple terms, the more thoughts of failure, loss, doubt, or victimization we indulge in, the more we act like victims and losers, and the more often we think these kinds of negative thoughts. By listening to what we say to ourselves, the mind sets up those experiences for us—like it's doing us a favor.

Since you'd like to have a better quality of life now, it's time to interrupt the conversation of negativity—to fight the fear you are living in and start on a fresh topic. Before you can go any further, you must use your Watcher to identify the specific fearful thoughts you repeat over and over again because of the loss you've experienced.

This is similar to the work you did in the chapter on plugging in; however, in this exercise, you're going to go deeper than just identifying negative words you use. You are really going to dive in to the negative thoughts that are playing in your head and look at the effects of them. Let's find the worst of these ideas, extract them, and replace them now.

1. Close your eyes and go deep within your daily memory bank. What is the biggest fear you have stemming from your loss? For instance, are you afraid of being alone forever? Are you afraid of going out into a social setting by yourself without your

spouse on your arm? Are you afraid of running out of money now that you're the sole provider in your family?

2. How often do you think about this big fear?

3. Do you see this fear becoming a reality anywhere in your life? Is it real? Be specific about where, when, and how this fear is manifesting, so you can start addressing it. Get specific about your needs so that your brain can be enrolled in the process of meeting them. Do you need someone to be with you at dinnertime? Do you need someone to go with you on vacation? Exactly how much money do you need to maintain your lifestyle?

4. What is the opposite of this fear for you? How does the opposite make you feel? If the fear is of being alone, then the opposite is companionship or sharing your life with someone. Let's say that makes you feel safe, peaceful, happy, or excited.

5. Now that you know the opposite feeling of your fear, I want you to say it out loud. Put your hand on your heart and say this word or phrase that is the opposite of your fear. How does your heart feel while you are articulating this?

Can this simple shifting exercise now help you to imagine the possibility of something great (the opposite of your fear) being a part of your life, regardless of the history of your loss? One woman who did this was

afraid of humiliation if she went out to a dancing event. Although she'd been afraid of rejection, when she got to question 3—"Is it real?"—she acknowledged that it was a projection, an imagined negative experience. She didn't actually know what would happen, because she hadn't tried yet.

To question 4 (What's the opposite feeling?) she replied, "Acceptance . . . celebration." She put her hand on her chest and allowed herself to imagine those feelings, and she felt wonderful.

Perhaps your experience was something similar. Did you relax or feel a bit excited? Did images come to mind of happy possibilities or positive outcomes that you'd like to experience?

Design a plug-in for yourself, based upon the emotion you discovered. What is one action you need to do to create an experience that will enable you to feel the way you want? (Remember, you only need to do an action that requires 5 percent of your energy, and no more. In other words, pick something small to do to give yourself this feeling.)

As you begin shifting your thoughts toward the direction of your new life, you'll need to ask yourself a very important question: *What do I desire?* After you're able to answer this question, you need to instill the truth that comes from having authentic experiences into your thoughts and emotions with the truth that comes from having authentic experiences with this desire. This is why I advocate for you to continue to do plug-ins.

If you answer the question, *What is my biggest desire for the life ahead of me?* when you are relaxed, even if that relaxation only lasts for a few minutes, you'll be more open to the possibility of a better life and more likely to feel hopeful that you can move in the direction of your future.

In this question, notice that I used the word *desire.* This word speaks to your heart. It will show you what your heart is craving. This intense desire is necessary for you to start the process of stepping out of the Waiting Room and into a world of possibility.

Identifying your fears, addressing them objectively, and looking toward the future will not only shift your thoughts away from your pain, but will also shift your identity from that of a person living with grief to that of a person living with life. These changes are difficult, but not impossible. Many people have done it.

I know you can, too.

Trust that your new identity is on its way and that the more shifts and plug-ins you create, the closer to you it will get.

SHIFTS TOWARD LIFE

During the last two weeks of December of the year following my husband's death, I cried, screamed, meditated, visualized, and found ways to use my brain as a tool to create a mental hologram of the new life I wanted for me and my girls. (This was right before I chased the mailman down the street.) At the time, I didn't know that I had entered the Waiting Room between the life before loss and the life after it. Although I had done much healing in the previous 18 months, I was still neglecting myself by working too hard. I still wasn't eating well and was isolated. I hardly ever picked up the phone when it rang. Even so, I was walking toward the doorway of my

new life one baby step at a time. Change had begun to take place within my brain. Though it wasn't reflected on the outside immediately, already I had started to shift my thought patterns from grief consciousness to life consciousness.

Evolving our brains in this way is no easy task, as it means we have to exit the infinite loop of thoughts about our loss that we've grown accustomed to moving through every day. We have to somehow rediscover our confidence in life, to believe that life is not over for us, so that we can indeed become Life Starters. At best, this is an awkward and uncomfortable process.

I'm sure that some people reading this book will think that shifting from grief consciousness to life consciousness is a theory, and that in practice, we'll perpetually grieve the loss of a person or an experience. Sometimes our guilt about detaching from the old life won't allow us to believe we can shift our identities. We also sometimes refuse to believe what we don't understand. But I can promise you, if this shift of frequency takes place in your mind, the pain and suffering of your grief will be replaced with memories. That resolution is part of the shift.

Maybe you've thought, *My loss cannot be understood by anyone else, as no one knows what I've been through. My own loss is so much bigger than anyone else's. Nobody can understand me.* I know these were the type of thoughts I had when I was starting over—and I've read thousands of comments online in which people were using these exact words.

Knowing that I'm happy today, people have said things to me like, "If I were as lucky as you are, then I would also be able to start over."

That always floors me. Was it luck that I didn't stay identified with my widowhood? Was it luck that I started my company, Second Firsts? Was it luck that I fell in love a second time and married a wonderful man? No, it was not luck. It was pure stubbornness and my determination to go against the current of grief and keep on fighting for my life.

Become a warrior and fight for your life.

Be stubborn about it.

Be determined.

Don't give up.

Your new life relies on you opening that door when she arrives.

Now that you have identified your negative thought patterns and consciously made a choice to focus on life, you must take actions to reinforce these changes. They don't just stick once you have done them—it is a continual process.

THE SCIENCE OF LOVE

As you are starting over, it is important to surround yourself with love—both from yourself and from others. Neuroscientists have discovered that anytime we feel safe, loved, and cherished, the brain releases small doses of oxytocin, the same chemical that floods our cells when we fall in love and helps a mother bond with her baby. Even when we just think about love, we're bathed in oxytocin. It causes a potent feeling of bliss and well-being.

In *The Scientific American Book of Love, Sex, and the Brain,* Judith Horstman explains that throughout our lives, relationships of all kinds are supported by oxytocin,

as it reinforces attachment and trust. "It's the hormone of love, trust, and attachment and is involved in every kind of human and mammal bonding. Unlike the hot spurs of testosterone and dopamine, oxytocin contributes to feelings of comfort and security."[1] That's why we should do our best to find ways to stimulate the release of oxytocin into the bloodstream.

But other recent findings about oxytocin are even more exciting to me because they have a direct effect on changing your brain and creating new neural pathways. As it turns out, if we are thinking about a memory that does not make us happy and simultaneously begin thinking about another memory that is happier, the juxtaposition of the two memories causes the neural pathways for both to begin firing together—permanently connecting them. If we can associate a negative memory with a more positive, loving, and secure memory, then it is less painful when it comes to mind in the future. This change, researchers have discovered, can be immediate, and it can be permanent.

The three shift actions that I've outlined here aim to use this knowledge in your favor. They use affirmations and visualizations to bring more love into your life and to help you strengthen your positive neural pathways.

I know that many of you are probably now thinking the same way I did when I first heard about the power of affirmations and positive thinking: *There's no way this can lift my grief and pain.* But when I discovered that brain science has proven their efficacy, my skepticism ceased. I felt I had no other option than to try it out and see if it would work for me. There was nothing to lose. My first attempt took place over a period of two weeks. During that time, I breathed and lived one affirmation: *I give myself permission to be happy.* For me, that was the ticket to so many of the second firsts in my life. Since then, I've never looked back.

Grief creates habits and beliefs in our minds that don't serve us. Grief's habits are egocentric and aimed at continuing the behavior we use to alleviate the pain of our loss. Pain often leads us to develop unhealthy attachments to things like food, alcohol, or television. These quick fixes numb the mind and distract us, but they don't lead to authentic happiness and success in life.

You're working now to let go of your unhealthy attachments and to establish a healthier attachment with your passion for a new way of living.

Shift Action 1: Affirm Your Shift

As you've learned, your thoughts create and strengthen the connections in your brain. Neuroscientists have a mnemonic phrase that can help you to remember and take advantage of this principle: *Neurons that fire together, wire together.* The reverse is also true. Brain connections go dormant if you stop indulging in patterns of thought that follow these pathways.

Shift Action 1 is designed to help you establish and reinforce positive links. Positive thoughts and feelings become more strongly linked—and more accessible—when you repeat them over and over again, and indulge in patterns of thought that follow life-oriented pathways.

Here's how to do it: If you catch yourself thinking about your loss in the "what if," "if only," or "I can't be happy again" mentality, deliberately interrupt your thoughts and start thinking about it as a memory. Your

loss is an event that took place in the past, and feeling sad, crying, and experiencing the loss through mourning is natural and healthy. But when it is done in a repetitive trancelike cycle, you strengthen the thoughts that will keep you inside the Waiting Room. Every time you interrupt negative thoughts about your loss, you break some of the links in your neural pathways that are connected to loss. Respond to those unwanted thoughts by striking back against them with a more accurate thought. You must absolutely reject the old idea. This is similar to what you did when the Watcher would break into the infinite loop of loss; however, in this step, you won't simply be looking at your life objectively, you'll be actively programming your mind for improvement, for moving into your new life.

To be convincing and maintain your freedom from the fear, doubt, or any other negative thoughts related to your loss, you need to react as soon as negativity comes up. Finding the positive thought pattern that you will use to counteract your specific fear is easy. You've already identified your biggest fear—the one that plays over and over in your head. You've gone through the work of proving that it is wrong when you look at it objectively. Or you've found the places that it may be manifesting. So all you have to do is take what you found to be your biggest fear and flip it. If you fear that you can't trust anyone, the opposite would be, "I am trusting."

Whenever your fear comes up, simply find a mirror, look yourself in the eye, and speak the opposite statement out loud with belief and strength. Remember that adding emotion to it and connecting with meaningful images related to this affirmation while you say it will heighten its positive impact.

It's also helpful to strengthen the positive pathways on a regular basis even when you're not reacting to a specific fear. You can use the mirror to help reinforce any positive qualities that you would like to see in yourself. This will make them seem more real and important to you. Try out phrases like the following:

- "I am open to love again."
- "I am welcoming life in."
- "I'm ready for my new identity to emerge."
- "I'm taking chances every day."
- "I can see the new me, and I am full of excitement about all the possibilities."
- "I'm here; I am in the present moment."
- "I am not ruled by my past."
- "My grief is only a part of me, and not the whole me."
- "I am starting over."

When tragedy strikes, we must strike back with a love bomb. If we repeat our suffering inside our minds by continually asking questions such as *What if? Why did this happen?* or *How could I have changed it?* then we integrate the loss more deeply within our identity. On the other hand, when we use affirmations to counteract our negative thoughts and create positive life-affirming perceptions, when we allow ourselves to feel their positive meaning in our bodies, we connect emotionally with those thoughts on a consistent basis, and then our lives change.

Shift Action 2: Love Yourself

With Shift Action 2, you're going to continue to strengthen the new positive neural pathways that you've been working on developing by connecting them with loving feelings. Love and gratitude are the most important things you'll need to feel in order to create the new life that you desire. This exercise will help you create an inner space full of feelings of love and certainty, as well as positive emotions about yourself and the future that you want and need to create.

You can do this exercise every morning if you wish, or just before you go out socially. If you will be giving a presentation at work, speaking in front of a grief support group, or heading out on a date, and the prospect gives you anxiety, this exercise will be helpful.

First, sit quietly and comfortably, slowly taking deep breaths. Relax your body. Begin using your breath to bring a pervasive sense of love into your whole being. You are safe.

With your permission, bring to mind the image and energy of a person you really love and care for. This person could be anyone with whom you feel safe. This person should be someone who always makes you feel good. It could be your partner, your child, your teacher, or your mentor. In your mind's eye, start going for a walk together.

Now imagine this caring person telling you exactly what you need to hear. For example, that you are capable and strong. Or that you will get a new job. Or that you're beautiful inside and out. Because this individual knows the truth of your character and your abilities, and wholeheartedly believes in you, when you imagine the person saying the words to you that you have requested to hear, you will feel nurtured. Allow yourself to feel love being given to you deeply in your soul.

If this person could describe your most important asset and how you need to use it every day, what would this person tell you? Imagine yourself being instructed by this loving companion. Listen to what he or she is telling you. Soak it in and savor it. This message is your truth. No matter the degree of fear you might feel about actually following the instructions you're given, this positive, loving experience can override the fear.

The purpose of this visualization is to create a safe space within you where you can go every day and communicate with the wisdom that lives within you.

Before you end the visualization, it's important to take a moment to feel grateful for the companion who knows you and guides you so well. Feel the kindness that your caring friend holds within his or her heart for you. Express your appreciation.

Then, claim yourself and the gifts you carry within. See yourself doing all that you have been afraid to do, and feel the emotion of this amazing new experience you're having.

Take a deep breath in and out, open your eyes, and come back to the present moment.

My dear Life Starter, if you begin crying when you do this kind of visualization, that's okay. Tears may come because the hidden dreamer inside you is listening and feeling love and support. These tears come from the fountain of your soul, from a place inside your brain that remembers who you are and wants to bring you forward into the life you deserve. Such tears are here to awaken the part of you that has the strength to ignite the fire of life dormant within you.

Often we are told not to bottle things up, but what does that really mean? Is it okay to bottle up your dreams and desires? Is it okay to suppress life? No, it isn't okay.

Uncork your dreams.

Shift Action 3: Find Your Breathing Space

If you're having a conversation with your grief even before you brush your teeth in the morning, it's a sure sign that you're still prioritizing grief over life. You're welcoming the new day with grief in mind. When grief is the first experience of your day, fear will join in. Grief is capable of providing enough reasons to persuade you that what you fear is real.

It's important to find breathing space in which to pay attention to life as soon as you are up. Grab a mug of coffee or tea and go where you can spend ten minutes alone and in peace.

Welcome to your breathing space.

This space you're looking for—the place where you are alone—isn't really a physical location; rather, it is a space within your body and mind that allows you to remove the weight of loss that you carry around with you. It is where you can consciously set loss aside and think about a better future.

A future where you feel alive and capable.

You feel strong.

You smile.

You are grateful.

You are compassionate.

You are loving.

Where is this place for you? If you recognize this place inside you, go there now. If not, find it. In your breathing space, you'll be called back to life. The more you practice finding your breathing space, the more the space will be with you all through the day, just a breath away if you need it.

SHIFTING JOE TOWARD LOVE AND SECURITY

In fall 2011, I started coaching an amazing man. Joe arrived at our first meeting with a big organizer in hand and a serious demeanor. He was ready to take action.

Joe was also reserved. He sat down and started talking about his goals with his face pointing toward the table between us. I kept looking him straight in the eyes, nonetheless, always behaving in a very caring and loving way toward him. "Joe," I said, after a little while, "I have such faith in what you will create in your life, and I am honored and humbled to work with you."

He looked at me with disbelief and surprise. "I bet you say this to everyone," he said with a big smile and a bit of a blush rising on his cheeks. Though he had deflected my compliment, he seemed to like it, and his trust in me seemed to grow. In the weeks that followed, Joe and I worked to build new neural pathways using positive thoughts and to enhance those he already had. Through this process, Joe opened up more and more.

It was fascinating for me to watch Joe alternating from being the person I first met to being a new person. One time I pointed out this alternation to him. "Joe, let me show you something that I've noticed. You tell me what you think." I then went ahead and mimicked his

grief persona. His body would curve downward on one side, and his voice would go very quiet as he spoke.

Adopting this posture and speech pattern, I repeated back to him what he'd just said, "Oh, Christina, I am sorry I come across like this. I find it so hard to believe that you think I have anything special to offer to this world. Maybe you believe this, but I don't think anyone else sees what you see." Joe immediately understood what I was referring to and laughed.

We had been working together for a while, and Joe had been diligently doing plug-ins. In my opinion, he was ready to make a major internal shift toward life. Therefore, I asked him to raise the level of his plug-ins to 50 percent, perhaps by going to a professional conference where he could find himself in the midst of other people who could see what I was seeing. At first he was very hesitant; he felt that he would not fit in with the people who would attend this kind of event. So at first I asked him to find his breathing space and truly think, from that place of strength, about participating in the conference.

His breathing space was actually talking to a good friend over a beer. The following evening, Joe went out for that beer with his best friend. This friend had been with him through all the tough times in his life. In the safe space that his friend created, Joe was able to see himself as a person who would go to this type of event. He booked his ticket that night.

Joe plugged in to his amazing new life for four days at the conference. When he came back, he told me, "I can't believe what I just experienced." His voice was strong, and he maintained a perfectly erect posture as he described what happened. "Thank you for helping me to see for myself that others will love who I am and value what I have to offer. Now I'm ready to take this to the next level." I could see that he'd made the shift necessary to start over. These days Joe spends his free time with his good friend while building a brand-new business that helps other people live life to the fullest.

Shift Now

If I had to do things all over again, I would go back to the years I spent grieving for my husband and take more risks. I would believe in myself more. I would make more time to play pretend in between episodes of my grief. I would dream bigger dreams for longer periods of time every day. I would find more time to spend in my breathing space, and I would reach out more often to the people who love me for support and affection. I would look in the mirror every day and tell myself how beautiful I am. I would speak to myself more—and listen, too.

Instead, I let grief monopolize my conversation during the first two years after my husband died. What a waste of time that seems to me in retrospect! For, in truth, this period of my life did not just represent me mourning my husband. This was me spending my precious days fearing a life without him. There is a distinct difference between these two ways of living.

Remember, grief doesn't have to be all tears and sadness. Your life after loss does not have to be worse than the life before. Actually, in my opinion, it can be better . . . because you'll have grown, learned about yourself, and evolved through the many tough days and nights of grieving.

Launching your new life after loss takes guts, bravery, boldness, and a lot of hard work, so be gentle with

yourself and trust the process. Remember, being a proactive Life Starter may be much harder than passively grieving for years on end and procrastinating about starting over, but the potential rewards are much greater.

Happiness.

Success.

Connection.

Excitement.

Message in a Bottle

Life Reentry can be a lonely experience.

Transformation into the person you want to be will require different kinds of losses than the loss you've already experienced.

The loss of relationships you used to have.

The loss of many bridges that connect you to the life you left behind.

It will almost feel like you are speaking in another language.

That is when you will feel it: *the loneliness of reentering life.*

Unexpected.

Surprising.

Yet necessary for your transformation to occur.

When we go through a devastating loss, a terrible life interruption, a broken heart, we find ourselves alone.

Evolution does not take place when our hearts break but when they mend. We get confused as to why we lose our best relationships during that time, *why we have no one by our side during moments of change.*

Please remember, you are on a different journey now, one that was unexpected and unplanned. The people who were with you in the past may find it hard to understand your new behavior. They may feel like they are losing you.

They will say that you have changed. They will be angry that you have no time for them.

But remember, it is not time that you do not have—it's *commonality*. Shared life experiences are no longer your connection points.

So stop trying to connect when you are met with resistance.

Let it be.

Go with the flow of your transformation.

Go with your truth about yourself.

You have other things to think about during this time. During this lonely, evolutionary time in your life, you must acquire new skills, possibly find a new career or a new job or a new love.

You must create a new relationship with yourself.

There's no time for guilt.

No time for shame.

Just time for breathing life again.

Life Reentry is not only an activation process, it's also a journey into the new self that is left alone to evolve and find its new tribe.

Some people will come along.

Others will not.

Be okay with that.

It is part of your reentry.

With evolution,
Christina

Chapter 6

LIFE REENTRY STAGE 4: DISCOVER

Somehow . . . I knew it was all going to be okay.
What I didn't know was that it was going to be more
than just that.
My future was going to provide me with one heck of a ride.
A life so unreal and so good that I often think I am
dreaming.

It is your birthright to feel alive, no matter what has happened to you.

You see, you were born with the capacity to live, love, laugh, dream, create, and play.

Now is the time to reclaim this ability.

I hope you are ready to discover yourself.

With your plug-ins, you've put your toe back in the river of life. But as you've tested the waters, you've heard the voice of your Survivor, the part of you that associates with your loss, telling you what you must do to be safe. The Survivor says, "I can't change . . . I can't do it . . . because something bad will happen."

As you know by now, your Survivor wants you to stay in the Waiting Room, so it can protect you from harm—forever. It is the source of your fear, and it has strong opinions about what is and is not allowable: You must not be "reckless." You must keep doing the same job. You may not begin dating until you've lost 40 pounds.

Its voice is very persuasive. It can give you reasons for every negative thought.

Experiencing life while you are still in the midst of grieving can be an exhausting process, because you have to contend with your fears and your doubts as you live. The Survivor, whose role is to remind you of danger and obstacles, may have seemed helpful, even necessary, at first, when the wounds of your loss were raw and you were mourning. But now that you are getting ready to let go of your grief for good and reenter life, you need the Survivor to step aside, be silent, and give you more space and permission to explore the world and express yourself.

In Stage 4, you will thank the Survivor for all its good efforts and ask it to take a brief vacation. Once it's gone, you're going to take your own journey into the past to find a place—usually a time in childhood—before you were ever touched by loss or pain. In this place, you'll reconnect with your unbridled, innocent, curious self— what I call the Thriver.

The Thriver is the dreamer in you who is full of vitality and desire to experience life. Yours may have been sleeping for years. Most people can very easily remember an event that changed them fundamentally from being a carefree young person to someone suspicious of life. For one, it was a public humiliation in the schoolyard. For another, it was the day her parents split up. For yet another, it was the day a beloved relative died in a tragic accident.

Whatever it was for you, this early trauma caused you to shut down a little or a lot. It ended your ability to trust the world as much as you did before then. That event in your past was when the Survivor was born.

In this chapter, I'm going to guide you to go back and reawaken the child you were before that day when you first got hurt, and to listen to what the Thriver has to tell you about happiness.

What's Happening in Your Brain Right Now?

As you know from having worked through the first three stages in the Life Reentry Model, on the physical level, your brain has been busy literally building a network of new neural pathways, so you can start to move past your grief. Emotionally, this has been experienced as a blend of highs and lows, life and loss.

Mentally, the emergence of new pathways is heightening your self-awareness. You have been developing insight, the skill of the Watcher. Instead of merely accepting your loss, you're now able to actively choose to think more positive thoughts.

On the spiritual level, you are questioning your place in the world. You are undergoing an evolution in how you live, love, and thrive. While we started this process in the last chapter by asking ourselves about our biggest desire for life ahead, we're going to dive fully into it now. We're going to define just what this life ahead will look like by looking into the past and the present.

Discovery is not a logical, rational process. It's something you have to *feel into*.

Being a "new you" can be a bit disorienting, as your brain is struggling to make sense of what's happening in your life right now and searching for new frames of reference. You probably feel as if you are on your own in an unfamiliar landscape and have no idea which way to go yet in life, because you don't even recognize yourself.

But you are not really an entirely new you. Inside the biology of your brain, you actually still contain all the versions of yourself that you have ever been.

Some of your neural pathways are going to sleep—becoming dormant or deactivated. Other neural pathways that were dormant are waking up—being reactivated. Finally, baby maps that have recently come into existence are being stabilized. And there is always a capacity to form new maps.

As you look to define your identity and imagine what the future holds, you can bring back valuable parts of yourself that you have lost or forgotten because they were ignored or suppressed.

The Thriver is one of these parts.

You need this capacity now more than ever.

The brain loves to run on automatic pilot. If you do not challenge your thoughts or give yourself something joyful to think about, the voice of your Survivor will be your pilot. By giving your Thriver a chance to speak its truth and by practicing listening, you can change your default setting.

The Bridge to the Past

A few years ago, I discovered that in order for people to reenter life after loss, I had to find a way to help them tell the story of their lives and losses from different points of view. When I asked them to describe their neural pathways, they would shut down emotionally. But if I helped them access the different parts of them that lived within their brains, and they allowed these parts, or personalities, to take turns telling stories, they started engaging in the process, and we started seeing results. Big results!

The Bridge to the Past, which is what I call this kind of storytelling, has since become one of the most important parts of the work I do with Life Starters. What it does is to help Life Starters build a bridge to the far past that bypasses the pain and anxiety of the present moment and recent past. It connects their happy past with their future.

Steven J. Siegel, M.D., Ph.D., from the Mahoney Institute of Neurological Sciences at the University of Pennsylvania, has done extensive research on the brain's ability to direct the mind toward different streams of experience.[1] This ability to direct the mind can open your eyes to all sorts of things you may never have thought about, things that could help you create a wonderful life.

Let me give you an example. Karen, whom I coached after her divorce, was having a hard time connecting to a possible future. When she did the Bridge to the Past exercise and I asked her, "When was the last time you felt like yourself, before you experienced a loss of any kind?" she transported herself back to a time years before her marriage when she loved to dance, and she rediscovered a long neglected source of joy. Reconnecting with her Thriver helped her see that dancing was an essential part of her happiness, and when Karen began dancing again after that day, she flourished.

If you look around, you may notice that many people in the world have lost the belief that life can deliver happiness to them. Even people who haven't gone through a huge loss often feel unable to create the lives of their dreams. One reason is that they have silenced the voice of their Thriver, which could help them see themselves as the masters of their lives. Perhaps you were like that before your loss . . . you didn't believe that your life could be great. I hope that since you have come this far with me, the tide of that belief may already be turning. That's what your plug-ins are designed to help you do ultimately: find real happiness.

Those of us who live with loss and go through a period of grieving are given a real opportunity to consciously choose how and where we will reclaim our happiness. This stage is where we choose to build a bridge to different mental maps that already exist within us, and to go back and forth between them until we discover in ourselves what we need to fully reenter life and step into our future.

Deep down, all of us already know our capabilities, our glorious perseverance, and our ability to thrive. We actually knew this a long time ago—and knew it with certainty. However, we too often deny knowing the truth about what makes us happy. In this stage, our goal is to verify who we were before we lost faith in life, so we can feel more hopeful and curious about the future.

Bid Your Survivor Adieu

Before we embark on perhaps the most important step in starting over, I must ask you to trust the process. Just stick with me, because what I'm going to ask you to do may seem scary.

Remember when you made fear your best friend? You appreciated it for all it was trying to do for you. Through that process, you were, in essence, befriending your Survivor. But now is the time when you have to take this friendship one step further—you must show your Survivor even more love, by setting it free.

This action causes a lot of people anxiety. Your Survivor has kept you safe for so long that you may not want to say good-bye. Even the suggestion scares some people. You may be worried that what I'm asking you to do here will cause you to break apart. You may be thinking, *Why would you want me to destroy the self that I've worked so hard to hold together?*

My answer is that I don't want you to break into pieces—and you won't!

I know how much you love or feel you need this part of you. The Survivor has been a good friend and has been with you even when nobody else was. It has protected you from all the pain and sorrow you were feeling. It has kept you company in the Waiting Room. Like your very best friend, it has been helping you live inside a safe routine. It is very protective of you. But to fully embrace your future, you have to learn to live without its constant protection. During your walk on the Bridge to the Past, I will ask you to say good-bye for now to the Survivor so you can have room to move forward and experience the joy, possibility, and freedom to choose a life that brings in the good experiences from your past. You want to make room for your Thriver. Your Survivor will always be there when you need it, but make it an acquaintance rather than a significant other.

Before you cross the Bridge to the Past, take a moment to send the Survivor to a safe place. Imagine it is being given a free trip to somewhere fun, warm, and relaxing—perhaps a place you'd like to go. Remember as you're doing this that your Survivor has been very good to you. As you're sending it on a trip, make sure to tell it how much you appreciate all its work. Acknowledge what it has done for you. Let it know that you are grateful.

Then let the Survivor speak to you. Is there some-thing it wants you to know before it goes on its way? Perhaps it wants to say "be careful" or "go easy on your-self." Just listen.

Having clarity about your relationship with your Survivor is fundamental to releasing it—just for now—so you can tap into other parts of your brain in preparation for your Life Reentry.

Finally, close your eyes and visualize the departure. Feel and see the Survivor going to the place you have chosen to send it on vacation.

How far away you send your Survivor depends on your level of comfort. One woman I coached sent her Survivor to a resort in the Bahamas for cocktails on the beach. Another sent her Survivor on a cruise through the Mediterranean Sea. Some people are very adventurous in their choice of destinations. One man, for instance, sent his Survivor to a faraway planet; creating this much distance was the only way he felt he would not hear it speaking to him anymore. People do giggle when they come up with a great place to send the Survivor for a rest. So don't be surprised if you feel a sense of joy in this release.

Once you've sent your Survivor to a safe place to rest, you are free to think new thoughts and dream new dreams, and you're ready to meet your Thriver.

Every so often, someone I work with wants to punish the Survivor. Some people feel mad for being afraid and getting stuck in the Waiting Room. One man—normally a very kind person—started swearing and yelling at his Survivor. The anger he felt toward his Survivor erupted when he realized he could separate from it. He felt the voice of his Survivor had stopped him from being the

man he'd always wanted to be. After he yelled, he apologized to me for being rude. We talked about it, and I helped him see that this part of him wasn't his enemy. It was only trying to protect him.

Remember, it's important to be respectful of this part of you and show it love and care, even as you ask it to step back. Your Survivor lives inside you and always will. But you are in charge.

I had a client who was only willing to send her Survivor as far as the next room. Her name was Kelly. She was a 55-year-old who had been living with her Survivor for about ten years. When her husband passed away, she became destitute. She literally had no roof over her head and no money to support herself and her daughter. They'd lived in a homeless shelter for a year while she cleaned houses and saved up to rent an apartment. Her Survivor had become very strong and felt absolutely necessary to her, so Kelly found it especially hard to let go. The most she could do was to imagine the Survivor taking a nap in the bedroom. But that was enough! Once the Survivor went to sleep, Kelly was able to travel back in time to find a part of her that she had left behind, a carefree young woman who dreamed of becoming a hairdresser.

MEETING YOUR THRIVER

Now that you've made room in your life by sending your Survivor on vacation, you're ready to get familiar with a new part of yourself.

Close your eyes and get comfortable.

Imagine that you are looking at a beautiful bridge right in front of you. This bridge is going to carry you back to a time in your past before you ever experienced significant hurt or loss. There you will meet your Thriver. I have wanted to introduce you to this part of you for so long, but I had to be patient, as I know that when the Thriver tries to come in too soon, it gets kicked out. Often Survivor thoughts are activated when the Thriver begins appearing.

Doing your plug-ins has helped you become ready to embrace the dreaming, life-loving part of you that is the Thriver. Because you've put some distance between you and your Survivor, you have enough mental space to reconnect to this part of you, which knows laughter, joy, and love.

See and feel yourself crossing the bridge and arriving at a time in your life when you had never experienced any loss, a time when everything was peaceful and happy, and you were blessed to feel alive. You may have been a child or a young adult. Remember your smile, your heart's desires, and your love for life. Go back as far as you need to go to find that time. Can you remember it?

If you can travel back through time and remember yourself and your emotions during this period, it will activate the part of you that knows how to thrive, be alive, and feel happy. In this exercise, I am asking you to become familiar with the dreamer self, the self that was an optimist and always thought of all the good in life that was possible.

What is a happy memory from when you were this earlier you? Remember smiling and how it felt to be alive in that time without loss, fear, or pain.

How old were you?

What were your thoughts?

Let yourself remember how you were during that time. Spend a few minutes living in the past.

Is there anything that you had forgotten about your happy self?

What was so fun about you then? Were you an artist, an athlete, or just a fun-loving kid who shared his or her world with everyone?

The you that you're reconnecting with is your Thriver, a dreamer, adventurer, and lover of life and people. The Thriver's heart is passionate. It wants to give and receive love.

What does this part of you look like?

If the Thriver could talk to you, what would it tell you? Listen.

Now invite this remembered part of you to come back with you across the bridge into the present. Can you feel yourself change as you walk? Are you walking with a different rhythm? Maybe your steps are a little faster, but not necessarily hurried. You're excited to feel this way again after such a long time walking heavily through your daily routine. Imagine the Thriver is taking you by the hand and wants to start running ahead.

As you arrive in the present moment, before you open your eyes, check in and notice how you feel. Is the feeling in your heart different than it was before? Can you see how this part of you was always here, waiting for you to remember it, acknowledge it, and experience it again?

Take a moment to bask in your feelings.

When you're ready, open your eyes.

BORN TO LIVE, LAUGH, AND LOVE

Your brain can regenerate, rebuild, reconstruct, and make new connections. Though you took a walk in your past just now, this part of you has always been with you inside your brain. If you have not walked through the neural pathways of adventure and life in a long time, it is because they were inactive. With this one simple discovery exercise, you just reactivated them.

Grief colors our lives in such an intense way when we've gone through a loss that the vibrancy of the world around us may be remarkably brighter after reactivating the Thriver. The thoughts you think when your Thriver has been awakened in your brain are the ones you need to practice repeating from now on if you'd like to change your brain's automatic, or default, setting. Yes, you have endured pain and hardship. But you were born to thrive.

It is okay to acknowledge that grief has gifts. It gives us depth and teaches us compassion. But it also draws the focus inward, away from creation and adventure. We need to be able to focus outward again in order to start over and fully reenter our lives after grief ends.

You are approaching this turning point now.

I have been fortunate to witness many rebirths of the Thriver through the Life Reentry program, and I always find it exhilarating. One in particular will always be in my heart.

Meet Tara. I remember Tara well because she underwent a remarkable transformation after reactivating her Thriver. When she started my Life Reentry program, she was in a bad state. She couldn't bring herself to get out of bed in the morning on days she didn't have to. She had been divorced three years earlier and was raising

two little girls on her own, a fact that reminded me of myself after I was widowed. Tara came from a family that valued academics, hard work, and making an income in a traditional profession, such as law, medicine, or accounting. She had therefore worked hard all her life as a nurse to earn money and make an equal contribution to her family's finances. Then, her divorce happened and the foundation of everything she believed was shaken. The values she'd adopted from her parents disintegrated. She had no principles to stand on.

There was something I noticed about Tara right from the beginning that intrigued me: her Survivor thoughts were, of course, strong. These kept her plugging away in her job and forced her out of bed in the morning. But her Thriver thoughts were equally strong. She always had one eye turned toward the future and the prospect of one day being happy again. She was fortunate to believe that her depression and disorientation were temporary.

I remember the week we met with her Thriver. She almost flew to embrace that part of herself. She went there so fast and so fully that she became euphoric. Almost overnight after that, her depression lifted. Letting go of her Survivor and reconnecting with the capacity of her Thriver to dream, she quickly began to open doors for herself and started to create an exuberant new life. This new life included a relationship that was very different from her marriage. It also included a nontraditional career path. She leapt at the idea of starting a photography business. Her Thriver neural pathways got stronger every day as she kept plugging in to her dreams, joyful activities, and creativity.

PLUGGING IN TO THE THRIVER

When people first discover their Thriver and bring that part of them back to life, they often experience a feeling of euphoria. However, their euphoria does not last long without assistance. It's like a bubble that bursts when they are no longer actively choosing to remember and connect with their Thriver. Your Thriver is like a potted plant: It won't survive if it does not get proper attention. All plants need water and sunlight. Your Thriver needs to be nurtured.

Once you meet the Thriver, you must remain in close contact with it in order to stabilize the neural pathways you've reawakened. For starters, design a small plug-in that you can repeat every day to reactivate it. This could be anything that celebrates or explores your dreamer self.

One way to keep the Thriver from going dormant is to put reminders of it in the environment around you. For example, you could get out some old photos of you that were taken during the early years of your life. Hang these close to your computer or in a prominent place such as on the refrigerator in the kitchen, where you will see them frequently.

You might also journal about your feelings while looking at the images of your happy self.

Do anything you can to keep the bridge to the past alive in your mind on a daily basis. In my work and my personal life, I've found three distinct versions of the Thriver that come through: the relationship Thriver, the creative Thriver, and the physical Thriver. Each one draws your attention to how to live your best life in one particular area, and each of these parts adds a different

dimension to your future life. Following are ways that I've found to plug in to each of these Thrivers.

The Relationship Thriver Plug-in

Keep stepping into your reawakened Thriver identity by plugging it in to your relationships. Was there a relationship that you loved having in the past? Do the Bridge to the Past exercise to connect with that memory.

What was so great about the person you loved spending time with?

What did you do together?

Look around you in your life today and see if there are people you know who are similar to that person you loved. If you are ready to step out of your comfort zone just a little bit, reach out to some people you would like to get to know better who embody similar qualities.

New relationships are not always easy to create, but if we practice forming them for 5 percent of the day, soon they will come to life. You could, for instance, send an e-mail to someone you have liked from afar. Or you could pick up the phone and call a new friend, if you feel up to it.

Remember that you shouldn't contact just anyone; make sure their essence aligns with the desires expressed by your Thriver. This isn't about reconnecting with life in general; it's about connecting with the life you want. Thriving in relationships is vital to creating a happy life. It strengthens our ability to create if we are surrounded by people who make us feel loved and happy. So please get out and show the world your thriving personality, and of course, introduce it to your thriving brain.

You will start to discover that you are bringing Thrivers into your life, people who match your new way of looking at yourself and your life. Start looking for the miracles of the Thriver inside you, and watch life be transformed on the outside, too, one relationship at a time.

The Creative Thriver Plug-in

After stepping into your new Thriver identity a few times, you'll feel a sense of greater inner permission to operate your life solidly from its point of view. As you do, you'll also see new doors open to you in the world, and there will be exciting and unexpected developments.

As you plug in to the Thriver, like Tara, you could find yourself being drawn to a new career or new hobbies and interests. It comes as a surprise to many people that each of us has a very creative side that can be accessed by plugging in to the Thriver.

Sensing the vitality of the Thriver often becomes a fuel that motivates people and overrides the fearful thoughts that the Survivor puts in their minds. Learning also overrides fearful thinking.

If you're inspired to create or indulge a new passion in your life, it is a good practice to make breathing room in which to do it. Ask your Survivor to take a nap or go out for coffee in Paris.

Put on your favorite music and connect with the vitality of your Thriver.

Then, explore your project.

Maybe this project is doing something new. Maybe it is doing something you have wanted to do for a long time and never got around to. Tara started taking photos with

her old camera and shared them with people in her life. This small creative plug-in brought about a lot of change.

What can you create that you can share with others?

Remember, your Thriver plug-ins require only a 5 percent level of input from you at first—nothing more than that unless you feel like it. As long as a part of you is thriving every day, then you are taking steps that move you in the right direction, toward your Life Reentry.

The Physical Thriver Plug-in

You will find that your body starts moving faster after you reawaken the Thriver. Even though grief is still with you and a part of you, you will start to move more and do more. Tap into your desire for movement as much as possible with plug-ins.

What exercise class could you take? When and where could you go for a walk?

In the beginning, see this plug-in as taking the Thriver "out for a walk" every day. The Thriver likes to be physical, as it has so much energy. You support and sustain your energy by letting the Thriver move every day. Think of this as bringing the Thriver into your body. The more tactile experiences you have with the Thriver, the more real this relationship gets.

Consult your doctor before beginning an exercise program if you have been inactive or have any medical conditions. But don't let the Survivor's fear of trying new things stop you. One of my clients started doing yoga after going through the Thriver activation process. It was a big deal for her because her Survivor had been telling her that she couldn't do any form of exercise due to a medical condition. She checked with her doctor, and he gave her the okay. Once she had her doctor's approval, she joined a yoga studio, and she discovered that her fears were erroneous.

The happiness I heard in her voice when she told me about doing yoga was amazing. "I never thought I could do this," she said. "I always believed my body would not be able to do the work." But it had not been her body that was unable to do yoga. It had been her brain. The Survivor was protecting her from any possible injury or hurt by shutting down this possibility. It is the brain's job to protect the body from threats. So watch out for protective, looping thoughts that keep you in the Waiting Room and away from your birthright to feel alive both in body and mind.

My Thriver

I must admit that my creative Thriver came to life before my relationship Thriver. I started to dream about creating Second Firsts and building a world of new beginnings much earlier than I dreamed of finding a new man to love.

My creative Thriver had been left behind in childhood, as my upbringing had to do with succeeding academically by getting good grades. Next to no emphasis had been put on using my creativity. To start over, I first had to tap into creation before I could fall in love. My intuition told me that I had to find my own voice before I could speak authentically to someone special. Second Firsts was created in my mind before it was created in reality. Spending time daydreaming about my future as the founder of a company brought me a lot of hope.

In my daydreams, I always saw myself as someone stronger, smarter, and more confident than I felt. I loved connecting with this future version of myself. I used to visit my Thriver every day, especially while I was doing the job in human resources that I did not like much. My Thriver gave me an escape hatch.

I believe that I met my husband, Eric, because of my creative Thriver self, even though I must admit the Thriver was at its weakest in that period. But still, the glimpses of the future the Thriver showed me were what made me want to put myself out there and try again to create, teach, write, speak, and love. As my connection with Eric became stronger, my relationship and my creative Thriver became stronger. I loved sharing my creative ideas with Eric, and this enjoyment helped me connect my internal world with the external one.

Over time, I was being aligned with a new reality, one that did not involve full-time pain. My Thriver helped me find hope again, and believe in my voice once again.

When I was young, my Thriver did not know how I was supposed to use its voice. It did not know that I would experience a loss and then reenter life with a stronger brain, heart, and voice. But that is what eventually happened.

My Thriver was surprised that I went back to find it. But it turned out that I had a better use for it here, today, than I ever did when I was younger. It helped me to reach this destination.

Your Thriver will take you on a journey to your new life, too.

I can see the bridge to the future waiting for you just on the horizon. Can you see it?

Message in a Bottle

It has taken me 40 years to discover how to *flow*, to understand the beauty of living with ease, the magnificence of singing in the shower, the divinity of walking a little slower and smiling for no reason.

Grief robs you of the ease of life. You forget that living can be easy.

Living can be easy.

You forget that feeling alive is your birthright.

And yes, I will admit this to you: I remembered this only very recently myself.

Can you remember what it feels like to have the ease in your life where good things happen out of the blue, where you are at the right place at the right time, and where everything just happens without you having to try, to struggle, to move mountains? With ease, you swim with the waves and move with the ocean's flow.

Can you imagine that?

Do you remember a time in your life when things were easy?

Let's go there together. Let's visit your past self and remember how it was to fall in love with the world, just because.

How it was to laugh out loud while standing in the kitchen.

How it was to play.

You see, my dear friend, you were born this way.

You were born to sing in the shower just because.

You were born to create spectacular visions and act on them.

But you have forgotten that living with ease is part of your DNA, part of being human.

Now how do we go from trying to move mountains to swimming with the waves?

I have to admit this is not easy. It should be, but it isn't.

The way I see it, the only way back to living in the flow is when you give up trying.

When you give up banging your head against the wall.

When you stop trying to change other people.

When you let go of the past and start living in the present.

When your future is not the bad guy you are afraid to meet.

When you let yourself burst into tears and let yourself scream out loud.

When you become yourself by doing what your heart desires.

Then life has no other option but to come back knocking on your door.

She heard you sing in the shower.

She saw your beautiful body swim in the ocean.

She met your heart through your tears.

And she felt your love for the people you could not change and chose to love regardless.

Life fell in love with you again.

She stopped trying to fight with you and moved right back in.

Will you do me a favor, and sing in the shower this morning?

With so much ease,
Christina

Chapter 7

Life Reentry Stage 5: Reenter Life

You can do the impossible, because you have been through the unimaginable.

The portal to a new life opens easily.

This portal can be activated in many different ways. I have seen it take place suddenly, like when a client experiences a shift from doing a certain plug-in or the Grief Cleanse. The brain molds itself to the demands of the lives we lead. Plug-ins, mindfulness exercises, affirmations, and joyful experiences will help you to discover aspects of the new self you are becoming. As these positive experiences begin to accumulate, they open the portal to your new life. They activate your laughter, your life, and your love.

At first, the avenues into your new life may seem insignificant, but I assure you they are not. They're important learning opportunities. If you experience a new feeling, a new idea, and a new force motivating you, your brain will do its best to adapt to what you are experiencing. The more life you feed your brain, the more it will build portals to your new life into your everyday routine.

When my brain saw me running to get my Christmas cards from the mailman and sensed how important this action was to me, it adapted by showing me additional opportunities to take back control in my life. A brain map was activated that day that I have come to view as the map of resilience and perseverance. This map was not entirely new. It had developed during years of fighting for my husband's life. What was new was applying my perseverance to fighting for my own life. My brain was gradually able to find what it needed inside my mind. Using preexisting brain pathways, it overrode the map of grief that my loss had established and opened the portal to my new life.

Finding the portal to a new life is difficult for some people, easy for others. It depends on their specific neural pathways. Regardless of difficulty, everyone is capable of reentering life.

You are capable!

Your brain needs to learn the route it can take to move you in and out of the Waiting Room between lives. Once it finds the route that works best for you, it will repeat the journey until the path is well marked and easy for you to travel. Knowing you can always retreat if you need to, your brain will then allow you to reenter life for longer periods of time. Finally, the reentry to life will become permanent.

During the reentry process, you need to remember that life has not killed your dreams. Grief did. Your brain did. Your loss of hope killed the dreams you once had.

Let me set the record straight. You must embark on your reentry journey by holding nothing back. You need

to give it all you've got. That's the way to come back to life and achieve your wildest and most exciting, productive, humanly connected, joyful, and all-around best dreams.

I know your perspective of loss is a bit different now than when you began reading this book. I know you've started dreaming again. Your next step is to feed the fire of life that's burning inside you. That's the step you're on.

Reentry should feel dynamic and life affirming. Though fear will probably be with you for a little while longer, and you'll have to dance with it while you're trying to create your new life, you must commit yourself to creating from your heart and soul nonetheless. Create from your passion, and your dreams will be more powerful than your fears. You must train yourself to believe in yourself more than you have ever believed before, for that's the way back to life.

Light up the world. Challenge the conversation that has been going on in your head since your loss. Let the voice of your passion be louder than that of your fear.

Put your hands on your hips, stand tall, look fear in the eyes, and show it that you've made a commitment to your dreams.

Set your old self free to find its place in your memories, not in the world you live in today.

RAISE THE BAR OF YOUR LIFE AFTER LOSS

This stage of reentry is all about creating your own destiny and walking through the portal to that life. I will ask you to set a goal for your new life—a big goal. Something that feels true to the person you have seen peeking out through this whole process. Without going through the stages of Life Reentry, you would not be able to set bigger goals for yourself. Without meeting the Thriver, the Survivor would be doing all your planning—and the Survivor is too uncomfortable with new or big goals to let you set them. But now your Thriver has made itself known. You've brought it out, met it, seen what it can do for you.

It's important to reinforce the Thriver in you by injecting laughter, adventure, and joy into at least some part of every day. Because of the work you've been doing with your plug-ins, you are more capable than you have ever been before. The Thriver is awake!

It is a huge privilege for me that you've read this far and allowed me to guide you to access more of who you are and to remember who you've always been, and I'm grateful for this. I believe in your power and creativity. I want you to know you can always take action on your own behalf.

If there could only be one thing you take away from this book, I would hope it is this: Even if you've just had the worst day possible, you can wake up the next morning and start over. You understand that you have within you everything you need to reenter life if you give yourself a chance to plug in and reflect on your thoughts and feelings, no matter what has happened.

You are the creator of your destiny.

I'm merely showing you an ability you were born with.

So I encourage you to raise the bar of your dreams. Dream big, and your life will grow bigger.

DREAMING A NEW DREAM

According to Rick Hanson, Ph.D., and Richard Mendius, M.D., authors of *Buddha's Brain*, "Mindfulness leads to new learning—since attention shapes neural circuits—and draws upon past learning to develop a steadier and

more concentrated awareness."[1] What they mean by this is that even after a devastating loss, our true nature of creation, evolution, and love will be restored if we pay attention to it and to our thoughts and feelings about it.

The brain is naturally adaptable and seeks balance. It also seeks to learn and grow. This is your Thriver waiting for you to explore life.

So I think it is time to set some new goals. I think you have finally raised the bar of life after your loss to where it needs to be. I know that deep down you are seeking laughter again; you are looking for joy and to be loved. I also know that you have started to believe that you can have what you want, no matter what has taken place in the past. Now, with a slight shift of the way you think, laughter is only a thought away. With just a small plug-in during your day, love could be around the corner.

Rediscovering yourself through the whole of yourself is an amazing process, but it is only now through your reentry that you can try and dream a different dream. It is now that you can set some new goals for your life ahead.

I have been waiting patiently for you to get here. As a coach, I wanted to bring you here first and fast, but I knew you would not be ready. Now you are.

You've connected to your present life and learned how to look at your thoughts objectively. You've figured out how to stop your infinite loop of negative thoughts. You've started to shift your thoughts from loss to life. And you've begun to explore your true essence by bringing back your Thriver, who has shown you what makes you feel alive, what brings you joy and hope, what makes you shine. Now you need to figure out how those activities and concepts will be translated into your new life.

The time has come to walk into reentry and see what is waiting for you. So it's time to set out a new big dream. Sit down with your notebook and start writing about what you want your new life to be. Make it as vivid as you can. Set out the place you will be, what you'll be doing for a job, the people you will be interacting with, what feelings you will live with. Write down anything you can think of that will make your life full. Make it everything you can imagine. Dream big. Remember, you are strong and creative.

NAME YOUR FIRST STEP TO MAKE YOUR DREAM REAL

Having laid out the new life you intend to lead, you can reinforce it by writing down a goal that you can take action on. Use the following six-step process to set the goal and record it.

Step 1. Start with a small new goal. Think of this goal as the younger brother or sister of a bigger dream you have. It's the first step you need to take. For example, if your dream is to get a postgraduate degree, then your small, first-step goal might be to fill out an application to be accepted as a student. You could call this goal "Complete Application." Think of it as a significant plug-in. It's a more elaborate and impactful action than a 5 percent plug-in.

These types of goals are the steps that will get you to the life you want in reality. Reentering life with a goal in mind is very important.

Step 2. Make sure you define your goal with precision, so your brain has a crystal-clear image of what it looks like when that goal is achieved. Will you be on the beach

when you achieve it? Will you be in a brand-new home? Will you have a graduate degree? How would your life look if this goal were achieved? Write the goal on paper from that standpoint.

Step 3. Once you have written down your goal, create an affirmation to support it, such as, "I am accepted at my dream university for fall 2014." Affirmations need to be written in the present tense, as if they are happening now. And they need to have a date by which they will be accomplished.

You know you've created a powerful affirmation if you feel emotionally connected to it. The words and pictures it evokes in you should energize you and make you happy when you say it.

It's important to shift your mind toward this goal and put your attention on it frequently, so repeat your new affirmation many times a day. Say it in the morning in front of the mirror before you brush your teeth. Say it in the elevator on the way up to your office. Say it in the car when you're picking up your kids after school. Say it before you close your eyes to go to sleep at night.

Step 4. Learn something new that relates to your goal. Expand your knowledge about your goal through reading books, conducting research, and interviewing experts. Ground it in reality.

Step 5. Manage your brain. If grief steps in and tries to take you back to the Waiting Room (where there is no fear, nothing to risk, and no danger), make sure you have a conversation with your Watcher and ask for advice. Your Watcher has the answers as to why exactly you might be getting pulled back to the Waiting Room and what you can do about it. You might also try doing another Grief Cleanse or doing plug-ins to strengthen your connection to your goal.

Step 6. Now let yourself have a blast with the prospect of taking action. Write down all the pieces you need to put together to reach your goal. Anytime we set goals, we suddenly discover that they actually have more than one facet. In "Complete Application," for instance, you may need to write an essay, gather financial information, ask for references, and so on. As you get clear on the actions to take and begin taking them, your goal will be achieved.

Drafting a goal is a means of stepping out of the Waiting Room and reentering life with a soft step. During this exercise, which could take you a few days to complete, make sure you take care of yourself and rest as much as needed. Starting to work toward achieving a new goal could not only get you some pushback from your brain, but also from your body.

As you define your goal, you may feel fatigued, get a headache, or feel antsy and distracted. Stick with the process, no matter what happens. Use your Life Reentry skills to counter fear and doubt. Remember, you've been through a very difficult loss and survived. Your brain is telling you to be afraid, but you know better. Reflect on your thoughts. Write. Journal. Then continue taking actions to move in the direction of your goal.

My Own Reentry to Life

I was in the Waiting Room for three years before I reentered life fully. My moment of truth came when I realized that although to other people I may have looked like I was doing well, almost everything I was doing felt wrong to me. I hated my job. I dreaded going into the office every day. Yet I'd worked so hard to land this job that I thought it would be a failure to let the job go and return to grief counseling. Had I wasted three years for nothing?

My fear was informing my professional decisions. It was telling me that I couldn't afford to leave my job, saying, *"You are responsible for your children. Quitting is an irresponsible decision. How do you know you'll succeed? How do you know you've got what it takes? At least here you've proven yourself."*

My realization then was that I was limiting myself. Nobody else was stopping me from doing what I loved.

Even though I was afraid to redefine myself, I made a decision to leave my job and pursue a dream of helping people start their lives over after loss. It took all the courage I could muster to walk up to my boss and tell her, "Two weeks from now, it will be my last day." My heart was beating fast at the very idea of leaving, because holding on to my identity in that office had helped me so much during my period of grieving. What was keeping me in that office was my Survivor, telling me that I needed the safety of that job to be happy, so I sent my Survivor on a really long vacation—but not out to an island to drink cocktails or on a cruise. I had to give my Survivor a job to do. It is out there keeping millions of people safe when they are in the throes of grief. Giving my Survivor to others who need it more was the only way my mind could let go of my own safety net.

The only trouble was that if I let the job go, where would I go next? What would my next identity be? I didn't have the answers, but I quit anyway. My Thriver was ready to lead the way for a while.

At that time, my company, Second Firsts, was only a two-word phrase that I'd written on a piece of paper one evening after dinner.

Nothing more than two words.

What does one do with two words?

Well, in my case, I took those two words and turned them into a paragraph that defined my vision for a company and a mission for my life. I started to see the bigger picture and to create a new world of Life Starters in my head. And finally the day came when the thought leapt off the paper and into reality. Then Second Firsts was no longer an idea or a thought, but a real entity.

Every step I took after that brought my company closer to being operational. I opened a bank account with $100. I got an e-mail address and a phone number that belonged exclusively to Second Firsts. Then, at a dinner party one night, I was asked the question, "What do you do, Christina?" *Oops!* This was the moment of truth, the moment for which I'd been waiting for years. In reply, I said, "I help people start over after loss."

"Oh, that's nice," was the response. The man who had asked me didn't jump up and down with thrills. He didn't notice my face changing color. He just moved on. But there it was: I was the founder and CEO of Second Firsts, just like that. My new company was real.

You might wonder if that was the moment in which I reentered my life. It was not. But there was one thing about me that was already different: I had started to believe that my life could change. I knew it was possible to experience a new beginning. I was still finding my way back to life, but after establishing my company, I was closer to being on the other side of grief.

I threw myself into working. Having quit my corporate job, I had to start selling my grief-coaching services. I remember my very first paying client. I wanted to frame the check as much as I wanted to cash it, so I held on to it for a whole week, just to admire it.

Despite that initial sign of success, running my new business felt very risky, so I would periodically retreat back into the world of my grief and hide. I had to learn to trust myself and persevere to start living the life of the new me.

I also remember when I first started to date Eric. The best word I can use to describe the experience is "frozen." During the first hour of every date, I'd sit as far away from him as possible in a very stiff and nonflexible physical state. I was very quiet and felt ready to leave in a hurry if I had to.

Was I really reentering life? Yes and no. My brain was giving me mixed signals. My first response was to run away, and yet my other, very strong response was to hope for a new life and to believe that something really great could come out of this brand-new relationship.

I wanted to leave my emotional Waiting Room so badly, but I was also very afraid to do so. What if I experienced loss again? What if this new person hurt me? And of course, guilt would also come in and talk to me, telling me that I was betraying my husband and my children by falling in love with someone else.

During those first months, I am certain that I came across as strong, fearless, and tough to Eric. But underneath that bravado, I felt very vulnerable. I must admit that I was falling head over heels in love with my future husband. I was indeed reentering life, even though fear was right there with me. Nothing could defeat me.

Part of me wanted to marry Eric immediately and fill the house with more children, get a dog, and put up a white picket fence. My Thriver was telling me that I was ready to fall in love and the time was right. It said, *"Embrace the experience."* Another part of me wanted to run away every moment of the day. My grief-stricken Survivor was not ready. I had to slow down and balance the conflicting needs of these parts in order for all of me to reenter life.

Life!

When I did reenter life one day, I experienced an electric jolt. My life, as seen through the filter of grief, had been so muted that once I started fully living again, my life felt vibrant. As I rediscovered myself, I saw myself as a different woman. Although I was still scared, fear no longer stopped me from doing the things I wanted to do. Once I started showing up for my life every day without resistance, I knew I had permanently stepped out of the Waiting Room and into the future I'd been waiting for.

An unexpected thing has been that my marriage with Eric is different than my first marriage. I am different in the way I love, in what I want from my spouse, and in how I show up every day. My first marriage was wonderful. My second marriage is, too. Nonetheless, they are different.

The biggest change of all has been the amount of gratitude I experience every day. I thank the Universe for

the life that I've been able to enter. Gratitude is a big part of my internal conversation and my thoughts. It shapes my beliefs. Having experienced the worst, I now know that what I have in my life is wonderful.

Periodically, my Survivor comes in and scares me by saying things like, *"What if you lose it all? Will you have enough money to bounce back? How will you take care of your heart if you lose Eric one day?"* But I have a lot of responses ready.

I am a Thriver, after all.

The automatic pilot in my brain today is set on fear-lessness. My fear centers get activated periodically, but not nearly as often as before. My beliefs have shifted enough to avoid setting off the alarm bells that used to bring my Survivor back to me and send me scurrying for safety. I am truly living inside my new life and well outside of my Waiting Room. Okay, maybe now and again I go back in there to rest for a little while. You can, too, but don't get too comfortable.

Promise?

We have talked about expanding your brain throughout this book, but I want you to know that your loss has also allowed your heart to expand in ways that would have never been possible otherwise. Because of your sadness, you have more depths in you to feel joy. Because of your tears, you have the compassion and sensitivity to mend other people's broken hearts.

During your reentry stage, you learn how to let go and to hold on. You learn first to grow and then to take a few steps back. Learning how to advance and retreat from life in alternation is an important part of the adaptive healing process.

If you've been working toward your reentry to life in increments, you may have already discovered how consciously placing yourself in loving environments and speaking about your dreams is the best possible way to support yourself to grow and evolve, whereas telling your story of loss and spending time with critical or discouraging people puts you right back into the drama of grief. By being mindful on a daily basis about what you say and do, you will eventually arrive at a crossroads beyond which you'll pursue a course in life that doesn't circle back on grief.

That's the sign you've made a successful transition into your new life.

Lisa's Reentry

She didn't notice her reentry right away. She didn't notice life's wind blowing through her hair that day. As she was so used to holding her head low to move forward against her challenges, she didn't notice that the resistance she'd been facing for so long was gone. She was so used to doing everything alone and having things seem like a struggle that she didn't notice when the difficulties dissolved. Lisa, one of my earliest clients, had no way of knowing that she had reentered her life, because she'd been living inside the Waiting Room for years—ever since her divorce was finalized—and she thought that she could only feel alive again if she fell in love. But her reentry to life, when it finally came, didn't arrive with a new relationship; it came with her experience of a state of flow and ease in her daily activities.

Lisa called me on the phone the morning she passed through the portal of her new life to tell me how everything she'd been longing for was suddenly happening all at once, and it felt so easy. She had just closed on a new house. For me, her sense of flow and movement was a sign of 100 percent immersion in life. During our conversation, she marveled, "How is it possible for all these good things to be happening with immense speed and so little effort on my part?"

In truth, Lisa's reentry to life didn't happen right when these positive events occurred. They were the result of her persistence at plugging in to life in ever-increasing percentages over a period of several months. The reentry had begun when Lisa started to take care of herself a little more every day, and it had continued when she replaced her habit of talking with her friends and family about her cheating ex-husband with conversations about her needs and desires. She was also getting ready to reenter her life when she giggled for the first time while watching a movie on her own.

For me, the ultimate proof of Lisa's permanent reentry to life, as her new self, was that the vocabulary she was using sounded different. Her comments in our coaching sessions shifted from "I have no way of knowing how to move on" to "I can see how it can get better." They shifted from "My home is where I shared my life with him" to "I am going to sell this old house as soon as possible and move so I can find breathing room."

While working with Lisa, I had made notes on how her vocabulary was shifting. Then I started reflecting her words back to her to enable her to witness how she was transforming. A reentry has to be seen and felt in order for hope to be born in someone who's had a traumatic loss, and for that person to develop belief in the security and stability of a new life.

In order for the brain to recognize the new neural maps it has formed, thoughts and actions must be repeated for at least several weeks and, in some cases, months or even years. This is necessary for connections between brain cells to be formed and then made stronger. It's also necessary for mindsight—the ability to observe our own thoughts—to emerge.

At first, when I would showcase Lisa's reentry to life, she doubted it and dismissed the proof I offered her. Fortunately, her doubts at that stage of her recovery didn't impede her progress. Her reentry was taking place, and her identity was gradually shifting along with her circumstances. The day she went into flow, she was finally ready and able to perceive it herself.

When I deliver my Life Reentry program, it's inspiring to watch a collective shift take place among the participants as they reinforce one another's progress. I feel a lot of joy in facilitating groups in shifting their language and their thinking, and taking very different types of actions on their own behalf. Time and time again, I've been privileged to witness the immense creativity that reentering life brings. Many of my program participants start new businesses. Some relaunch careers they abandoned years earlier. All investigate their life purpose and come to conclusions about their identities that they wouldn't have arrived at without their losses.

Lisa was a private client, rather than a group member, but she went through the very same process that people in my groups do. During the early steps of her reentry, she began to immerse herself in an art class and painted the most amazing landscapes and still lifes. The idea of producing an art exhibit, as a labor of love, gave her hope and raised her confidence. Becoming an artist caused her brain to form the baby neural pathways of a very dynamic new personality. Since our brains learn mainly from what we pay attention to, we can surmise that Lisa's brain started to change when she tended to herself, her skills, and her profession.

Lisa was diligent in doing the exercises I gave her. She practiced mindfulness. Every night she got real about her grief and wrote about what was going on inside her in a journal. She reflected on her grief and also on the different dimensions of her life. She practiced plug-ins, and as a result started to create new types of experiences. She purposefully dated men who were very different in personality from her former husband in order to break the paradigm of her unhappy marriage. Mindfulness was the tool that increased her awareness of her behavior sufficiently to help her break free of old negative patterns.

Through her months as a Life Starter, Lisa experienced different brain states, including happiness, love, and joy, which brought her to a brand-new place—a place outside the infinite loop of loss of her former identity as a divorced woman. Her brain was able to learn to live a new life by creating baby neural pathways that eventually matured and overrode the maps that were not serving her. She let the old neural pathways go dormant by ignoring them. She conditioned her brain by giving herself rewards for taking steps to live her life, instead of for grieving. Experiencing love for herself and her activities enabled her to bring people into her life who supported her and admired the goals she was setting. Switching jobs put her into a very different workplace than that of her old job. In this new environment, she was encouraged to tap into her creativity.

At the end of her marriage, Lisa had forgotten who she was and had lost track of her desires due to the depth of grief she felt. As Lisa's brain integrated all of the elements I have just described, she learned which of her neural pathways were better for bringing her back to her natural state of being.

THE DOOR TO YOUR REENTRY

At the beginning of this chapter, you created a new life plan and set out some goals to help you work your way toward it. Now it's time for a very intense exercise that will bring together everything you have gone through so far. It is a guided visualization with your Thriver leading the way. It will help you open the portal and pass through into your new life.

You can do this exercise on your own, or you can have someone read this section of the book to you. Either way, look forward to your reentry.

Close your eyes, sit comfortably, and breathe in and out. Imagine you are about to reenter LIFE.

Visualize a door in front of you.

What does it look like?

Is it large or small?

Is it heavy or light?

Is it white, brown, or another color?

Really see it.

This is the door to your new life—the life you have been waiting to have. This life has also been waiting for you while you were in the Waiting Room.

Once you can see the door, imagine yourself putting your hand on the handle or doorknob. Really allow yourself to feel it in your hand. Hold on to it tightly.

Now push the door open and look beyond it.

As you step through the doorway, know that your Thriver is leading the way. Your Thriver is holding your hand and walking through the doorway with you.

Your Watcher is right beside you, too, as always, observing your every move.

The Survivor stays behind. It knows to stay in the Waiting Room until you need its support again. It knows its place.

Think back to the ideal life you laid out. This is what's in front of you now.

As you enter your new life, take a look around. Can you see what's beyond the threshold?

Is the new life light and bright, cozy and comfy?

Do you see an ocean or mountains?

See yourself. Observe your actions.

What are you doing?

What are you wearing?

How does your hair look?

Are you standing, or are you sitting?

Are you relaxed?

What's in front of you?

What are you looking at in this new life?

Who is there with you? What do they look like, and what are they doing?

What is the creative dream that you're making come true?

What resources do you have with you to make it real?

You have help. You are not alone. Who is helping you make this dream come true?

What plug-ins have you already completed that make this goal possible?

Observe what it is like for the goal to be realized.

Now you can see someone who loves and cares about you. Do you see them with you? If this person has not yet arrived in your life, just allow yourself to imagine someone and start seeing them right there. What are their features? How do they look?

Let your brain create a new map with your Thriver in charge. Your Thriver wants to bring you love, hope, and the brand-new relationship that you deserve because of who you are.

In this new life, you feel knowledgeable and ready to take chances, because you know you have survived the worst and made it to the other side. You are different: stronger, better, and wiser than you were in the past. You have many qualities inside you that you can build upon.

If there is any doubt in your mind, it belongs to the Survivor outside the door. Hear how far away those doubts are. Such ideas are not coming from the Thriver.

Hear the Thriver speaking to you right now, telling you that you can do this.

> *You're so ready.*
> *You've been ready for a long time.*
> *This is your chance. This is your time.*
> *In this new life, you are ready to make your dreams come true. You are ready to love again, laugh again, and live fully!*
> *You should not care what other people think or what they say, as they have not walked in your grief shoes. They do not know what you've been through. They can never know, so don't expect them to.*

Your Thriver is in charge and knows what you can create because of the new map of reentry.

Think about your new goal, your new dream.

Sometimes when we're trying to create a goal, guilt likes to come in, saying we don't deserve it. Grief says, "What about me?" So you are going to create someplace special for guilt and grief to live.

Look to your left and you will see a beautiful path that leads to a little house. Situate this house wherever you like. This is where your guilt and grief will live from now on. Now they can come visit you—with your permission. And you can go visit them, knowing that the way back to your new life is an easy path to follow. You have nothing to worry about. You can return to your new life whenever you want.

Leave guilt and grief in the house now and follow the path back to your dream life.

Before you finish this visualization, repeat your new goal several times: "I am going to create (*fill in the blank*) for myself because I deserve it and I want to live my life fully."

When you're ready, open your eyes.

GIVE YOURSELF TIME—REENTRY IS A PROCESS

Right now, you have a grand opportunity to create a life that pleases you. You can bring back aspects of life that you've abandoned, if you want. You can test out a variety of ideas that seem interesting. Explore. Investigate. Use your curiosity. Play. Follow your instincts and impulses. You can't do it wrong. Your life will be whatever you make of it. Nothing more, nothing less.

Having observed the behavior of thousands of Life Starters, it's clear to me that the same types of losses, experienced at the same level of devastation, are processed differently by each person who grieves a loss. You may need counseling before you undertake the action-based approach to starting over after loss. Your emotional needs depend on your history, your personality, and how recently your loss occurred. However, once you've processed your grief, your brain will be ready for you to reenter life. As a Life Starter, use this stage in the Life Reentry Model as your launchpad to create a beginning for your brand-new life. The doorway you step through will open when you're ready.

Reentry doesn't mean we forget those we once loved or forget our pain.

It means we remember how to live.

Message in a Bottle

Throughout my life, I always saw people as better than I was. I believed they knew more than I did, had better brains, were more cool, and somehow had it more together.

In the last few years, I've learned something that took me by surprise.

All of the above was inaccurate.

I am actually quite the woman.

Very smart.

Extremely fast.

With a darned big heart.

I started seeing myself for the first time as I really was: a true warrior, a spectacular soul who had a very special journey ahead of me. And that is when it all started to unfold.

Dreams leapt from my imagination into my reality.

Love came back.

Work became divine.

At the end of it all, I learned that nobody is better than I am. I had just been seeing myself from a place of weakness, from a place of fog.

I share all this because I know a lot of people are exactly where I was all those years ago.

I want you to know this: you are spectacular beyond your wildest dreams.

Nobody could ever do what you are here to do.

If people look down on you, look up at the stars, because that is where your home is.

When you see yourself as less, know that you are more than you see and more than you know.

You have to trust that quiet voice of the Thriver, who has been telling you there is more for you.

Believe it.

This voice comes from your soul's journey.

It speaks the truth.

I see you.

I know who you are.

Now, in order for this to work out, you have to start seeing what I see in you.

And the world will change.

Forever.

With faith and trust,
Christina

Conclusion

WELCOME BACK!

Ultimately, living a truly unapologetic life is about being proud to feel alive after a terrible loss. It's about being able to tell guilt that it's time to leave, because you're ready to reenter your life and start living again. It's about standing tall, being confident, and wearing your wounds as badges of having lived a life.

You are truly here.

You made it.

You got real with your grief, you plugged in to the life you wanted, and you shifted while discovering your new self. You traveled the distance from your loss to your new life. You've experienced the energetic evolution that takes place after a dramatic life interruption or a broken heart.

Your loss has allowed your character, your brain, and your personality to change. Therefore your needs, dreams, wants, and aspirations have also shifted. Now your whole world can be viewed and interacted with from a whole new perspective and higher level of insight.

I truly believe that one day everyone in the world will wholeheartedly embrace the fact that loss creates a kind of disequilibrium within us. That it changes everyone and everything in our lives—and quite possibly for the better, after equilibrium is reestablished. It may take some time before the world is open to considering this idea, but I hope that this book has unlocked a small door of belief in your mind, one that you can squeeze through and create a brand-new beginning.

I welcome you back to the land of the living, and in a sense, I am welcoming the new you, the new version of yourself that has never been here before. You just gave birth to someone who could not have made it this far without experiencing loss and pain. This new you no longer doubts that you have the ability to create the life you want. This new version of you doesn't listen to fear. The new you doesn't apologize for the mistakes and tears or for the successes and the laughter. This new you is ready to leap and create an even bigger life than the one that was left behind.

I believe that your future will give you the proof you need to believe in your own healing through action, shifts, and taking true steps toward a fully lived life. I believe that your launchpad will create the second firsts that you deserve after such a loss.

Always remember to believe in your brain's ability to guide you back to your life.

Yes, life holds heartache. I can't pretend that isn't true. Life will break your heart again after you have reentered it. Your heart could break for a second time, or for a third and a fourth time.

But then life and your brain can mend your heart again. Just remember to use the reentry process to build a new launchpad every time you go through a loss.

Break. Mend.

Break. Mend.

Break.

Mend.

Sadly, sometimes the mending will not follow breaking for quite a while—not because it can't, but because broken hearts can remain forever broken. Being broken, as you know by now, can become habitual if we don't consciously choose to go through the steps to reenter life.

As time goes by, after you have set down this book, your brain might want to go back to its old habits. Be careful not to let this happen. Your heart can't evolve if you rely on those habits.

It can't participate.

It can't contribute.

It can't be compassionate.

It can't love authentically.

It can't believe.

Your soul can't create when you're in a broken state.

Most people whose hearts have been broken for a long while are convinced that they cannot reconstruct themselves or start over. They believe that they have lost the capacity to mend. I'm here to welcome you back, if you've had those doubts, with a strong reminder: Mend and reenter whenever you have to, by starting to plug in to life and moving through your second firsts.

As you know, when my husband took his last breath, I thought my heart would never be put back together again. There were too many pieces to bring back, too many pieces to find them all. As you saw, my heart went on a journey in search of the missing pieces so it could mend itself. During this journey I discovered a different way of mending a broken heart.

Mending is the ability to reenter life with a broken heart, while it's getting fixed. Mending does not mean that the heart will be as good as new. Just that it can beat again . . .

Love again . . .

Play again . . .

Act again . . .

Speak the truth again . . .

Feel again . . .

Laugh again.

That is when mending is complete.

Some pieces of your old life will not be found. They have been scattered across the universe. But don't worry. Your heart will give birth to new pieces that are similar to the ones that you lost. It gives birth to these pieces since the pieces of your original heart can never be restored.

The new pieces of your heart are stronger and wiser.

While I welcome you back to life, I also want to let you know that the new you was born from your story of loss. Every cell in your body changed when your heart broke. Without your time of mourning, the river of life would not have run through you and brought you to where you are now. You would not be you, as you are today, without it.

Yes, I am talking about your tears . . . the tears you cried. As you were able to let them flow, they changed your life, they changed your soul, and they changed your destiny.

Those tears were meant to be cried before you could reenter life and before you could discover what you have discovered about yourself. This river arrived at the beginning of your grief to cleanse you of sorrow, to make you stronger, and to help you evolve your soul.

You do not need to try to stop the river even after you have reentered your life. Tears may continue to fall upon occasion, but you are back. You are back to living outside of the cloud of grief, ready to take on life and live it fully.

Welcome back.

Life is waiting for you.

Go live it.

RESOURCES FOR LIFE STARTERS

Programs to Help You
Start Over after Loss

Christina created the following programs to provide you with additional support as you move through the Life Reentry Model.

Second Firsts Message in a Bottle Newsletter

You can subscribe to this life-changing weekly newsletter for free by visiting SecondFirsts.com.

Second Firsts Reentry to Life Program

The Reentry to Life program is a live distance coaching course that combines revolutionary neuromapping and reprogramming techniques, compassionate personal coaching, and assignments designed to help break the cycle of mourning and clear space for new visions and goals. It includes downloadable Life Ignition audio sessions and companion workbooks, each devoted to the stages of Life Reentry. Visit SecondFirsts.com.

Second Firsts Life Ignition and Business Ignition Coaching Sessions

If you would like individual attention, personal Life Ignition and Business Ignition coaching sessions are available. These are designed to help you gain insight into your life and discover your own natural ability to move forward in your life or in your career. Visit SecondFirsts.com.

Join the Community at TheLifeStarters.org

TheLifeStarters.org is an action-oriented social network that utilizes the Life Reentry Model to help people take steps to start over after loss, natural disaster, personal crisis, illness, job loss, and war. It is built with extraordinary peers, volunteer coaches, and resources and tools that have reignited thousands of lives. This is about breaking the cycle of grief by training your brain to reward you for your bravery, compassion, and forward momentum.

Connect with Christina and Second Firsts on the Social Networks

Connect directly with Christina on the social networks. Meet Christina on Facebook at Second Firsts. Follow her on Twitter @secondfirsts and @thelifestarters. Also connect with her on LinkedIn, Google+, and Pinterest as Christina Rasmussen.

For more information on these and other programs
and opportunities, please visit
www.SecondFirsts.com
www.TheLifeStarters.org

RECOMMENDED READING FOR LIFE STARTERS

You may find the following books helpful
in your journey of Life Reentry.

General Books on Grief

George A. Bonanno, Ph.D. *The Other Side of Sadness: What the New Science of Bereavement Tells Us about Life after Loss.* New York: Basic Books, 2009.

Joan Didion. *The Year of Magical Thinking.* New York: Alfred A. Knopf, 2005.

C. S. Lewis. *A Grief Observed.* New York: HarperOne, 2001.

Susan Piver. *The Wisdom of a Broken Heart: An Uncommon Guide to Healing, Insight, and Love.* New York: Free Press, 2010.

Bernie S. Siegel, M.D. *Buddy's Candle.* Bloomington, Indiana: Trafford Publishing, 2008.

Books on the Brain

Daniel G. Amen, M.D., and David E. Smith, M.D., *Unchain Your Brain: 10 Steps to Breaking the Addictions that Steal Your Life.* Fairfield, CA: MindWorks Press, 2010.

Miriam Boleyn-Fitzgerald. *Pictures of the Mind: What the New Neuroscience Tells Us about Who We Are.* Upper Saddle River, NJ: FT Press, 2010.

Deepak Chopra, M.D., and Rudolph E. Tanzi, Ph.D. *Super Brain: Unleashing the Explosive Power of Your Mind to Maximize Health, Happiness, and Spiritual Well-Being.* New York: Harmony, 2012.

Antonio Damasio. *Self Comes to Mind: Constructing the Conscious Brain.* New York: Pantheon, 2010.

David DiSalvo. *What Makes Your Brain Happy and Why You Should Do the Opposite.* Amherst, NY: Prometheus Books, 2011.

Norman Doidge, M.D. *The Brain that Changes Itself: Stories of Personal Triumph from the Frontiers of Brain Science.* New York: Penguin, 2007.

Rick Hanson, Ph.D., and Richard Mendius, M.D. *Buddha's Brain: The Practical Neuroscience of Happiness, Love, and Wisdom.* Oakland, CA: New Harbinger Publications, 2009.

Judith Horstman. *The Scientific American Book of Love, Sex, and the Brain: The Neuroscience of How, When, Why, and Who We Love.* San Francisco, CA: Jossey-Bass, 2011.

Sonja Lyubomirsky. *The How of Happiness: A New Approach to Getting the Life You Want.* New York: Penguin, 2007.

John Medina. *Brain Rules: 12 Principles for Surviving and Thriving at Work, Home, and School.* Seattle, WA: Pear Press, 2009.

David Perlmutter, M.D., F.A.C.N., and Alberto Villoldo, Ph.D. *Power Up Your Brain: The Neuroscience of Enlightenment.* Carlsbad, CA: Hay House, 2011.

Srinivasan S. Pillay, M.D. *Life Unlocked: 7 Revolutionary Lessons to Overcome Fear.* Emmaus, PA: Rodale, 2010.

Jeffrey M. Schwartz, M.D., and Sharon Begley. *The Mind and the Brain: Neuroplasticity and the Power of Mental Force.* New York: ReganBooks, 2002.

Daniel J. Siegel, M.D. *The Developing Mind: How Relationships and the Brain Interact to Shape Who We Are.* New York: Guilford Press, 1999.

———. *Mindsight: The New Science of Personal Transformation.* New York: Random House, 2010.

C. Alexander Simpkins and Annellen M. Simpkins. *The Dao of Neuroscience: Combining Eastern and Western Principles for Optimal Therapeutic Change.* New York: W. W. Norton and Company, 2010.

178

Books on Spirituality

Deepak Chopra, M.D. *The Seven Spiritual Laws of Success: A Practical Guide to the Fulfillment of Your Dreams.* San Rafael, CA: Amber-Allen Publishing, 1994.

Mike Dooley. *Choose Them Wisely: Thoughts Become Things!* New York: Atria, 2009.

Wayne W. Dyer, Ph.D. *Change Your Thoughts, Change Your Life: Living the Wisdom of the Tao.* Carlsbad, CA: Hay House, 2007.

———. *Excuses Begone! How to Change Lifelong, Self-Defeating Thinking Habits.* Carlsbad, CA: Hay House, 2009.

———. *Wishes Fulfilled: Mastering the Art of Manifesting.* Carlsbad, CA: Hay House, 2012.

William Gladstone, Richard Greninger, and John Selby. *Tapping the Source: Using the Master Key System for Abundance and Happiness.* New York: Sterling Publishing, 2010.

Louise L. Hay and Cheryl Richardson. *You Can Create an Exceptional Life.* Carlsbad, CA: Hay House, 2011.

Louise L. Hay. *You Can Heal Your Life.* Carlsbad, CA: Hay House, 1999.

Esther Hicks and Jerry Hicks. *Ask and It Is Given: Learning to Manifest Your Desires.* Carlsbad, CA: Hay House, 2004.

———. *The Law of Attraction: The Basics of the Teachings of Abraham.* Carlsbad, CA: Hay House, 2006.

Mark Matousek. *When You're Falling, Dive: Lessons in the Art of Living.* New York: Bloomsbury Press, 2008.

Judith Orloff, M.D. *Emotional Freedom: Liberate Yourself from Negative Emotions and Transform Your Life.* New York: Three Rivers Press, 2009.

Osho. *Courage: The Joy of Living Dangerously.* New York: St. Martin's Press, 1999.

Eckhart Tolle. *A New Earth: Awakening to Your Life's Purpose.* New York: Plume, 2005.

———. *The Power of Now: A Guide to Spiritual Enlightenment.* Encinitas, CA: New World Library, 1999.

Books on Career and Success

Charles Duhigg. *The Power of Habit: Why We Do What We Do in Life and Business.* New York: Random House, 2012.

Chris Guillebeau. *The Art of Non-Conformity: Set Your Own Rules, Live the Life You Want, and Change the World*. New York: Perigee, 2010.

Anthony Robbins. *Awaken the Giant Within: How to Take Immediate Control of Your Mental, Emotional, Physical and Financial Destiny!* New York: Free Press, 1991.

David Rock, Ph.D. *Personal Best: Step by Step Coaching for Creating the Life You Want*. East Roseville, NSW, Australia: Simon and Schuster Australia, 2001.

Books on Health

Kris Carr. *Crazy Sexy Diet: Eat Your Veggies, Ignite Your Spark, and Live Like You Mean It*. Guilford, CT: Globe-Pequot Press, 2011.

———. *Crazy Sexy Kitchen: 150 Plant-Empowered Recipes to Ignite a Mouthwatering Revolution*. Carlsbad, CA: Hay House, 2012.

T. K. V. Desikachar. *The Heart of Yoga: Developing a Personal Practice*. Rochester, VT: Inner Traditions, 1999.

Mark Hyman, M.D. *The Blood Sugar Solution: The UltraHealthy Program for Losing Weight, Preventing Disease, and Feeling Great Now!* New York: Little, Brown and Company, 2012.

Jared Koch with Jill Silverman Hough. *The Clean Plates Cookbook: Sustainable, Delicious, and Healthier Eating for Every Body*. Philadelphia, PA: Running Press, 2012.

Mark Lauren with Joshua Clark. *You Are Your Own Gym: The Bible of Bodyweight Exercises*. New York: Ballantine Books, 2011.

Notes

The Science of Getting Past Grief

1. Jeffrey M. Schwartz, M.D., and Sharon Begley, *The Mind and the Brain: Neuroplasticity and the Power of Mental Force* (New York: ReganBooks, 2002).

2. Linda Graham, M.F.T., "Skillful Ways to Deal with Stress and Trauma," originally published in *Wise Brain Bulletin*, Volume 3.4 (2009). Website: http: lindagraham-mft.net.

3. C. S. Lewis, *A Grief Observed* (New York: HarperOne, 2001): p. 15.

4. Daniel J. Siegel, M.D., *The Developing Mind* (New York: Guilford Press, 1999): p. 215.

5. John Medina, *Brain Rules* (Seattle, WA: Pear Press, 2009): p. 31.

6. Ibid: p. 32.

Life Reentry Stage 1: Get Real

1. David DiSalvo, *What Makes Your Brain Happy and Why You Should Do the Opposite* (Amherst, NY: Prometheus Books, 2011): p. 13.

2. Daniel J. Siegel, M.D., *Mindsight* (New York: Bantam Books, 2010): p. ix.

3. Deepak Chopra, M.D., and Rudolph E. Tanzi, Ph.D., *Super Brain* (New York: Harmony, 2012): p. 16.

Life Reentry Stage 3: Shift

1. Judith Horstman, *The Scientific American Book of Love, Sex, and the Brain* (San Francisco, CA: Jossey-Bass, 2011): p. 23.

Life Reentry Stage 4: Discover

1. Steven J. Siegel, M.D., Ph.D., "Mindfulness Training and Neural Integration: Differentiation of Distinct Streams of Awareness and the Cultivation of Well-Being," in *Social Cognitive and Affective Neuroscience,* vol. 2, no. 4 (2007): pp. 259–63.

Life Reentry Stage 5: Reenter Life

1. Rick Hanson, Ph.D., and Richard Mendius, M.D., *Buddha's Brain* (Oakland, CA: New Harbinger Publications, 2009): p. 14.

ACKNOWLEDGMENTS

I would like to thank my husband, Eric Tinker, who believed in me before anyone else. Without his love and daily support, Second Firsts would not have been possible. Thanks also to my beloved daughters, Elina, Isabel, Lindsay, and Lauren, for their unconditional love and enthusiasm.

To my parents, Nikos and Despina, for teaching me not only to have big dreams, but also to act on them. Had it not been for their vision of me, my own vision of myself could not have been as big as it is. I also have deep appreciation for my sister, Artemis, for always knowing my path, even before I do.

This work would not be possible if I had not experienced many life interruptions and devastating losses, especially losing my first husband, Bjarne, tragically to cancer in 2006. He inspired me to live fully and to take action toward my dreams. He fought for his life every day, and he treasured every minute he had with us. I promised him that I was to live two lives in my one after his death. This book is part of my quest not only to live fully, but also to help others bring back the joy in their lives after loss.

I am indebted to the Children's Room in Arlington, Massachusetts, for providing a safe haven for me and my children while we were recovering from our loss.

A few friends deserve special mention for the support they gave me when I was starting over: Shannon Amsler and Nathalie Dolicy and Trudy Cairns. Thank you.

For all the days that my body did not want to move forward, I am grateful to master personal trainer Linnea Molgard for helping me take care of myself, but most of all for listening to my constant chatter about the book. You are an angel on earth.

I am eternally grateful to my friend and editor, Stephanie Gunning, for her relentless quest for flow and simplicity, and for seeing the value of my work even before the book was written. I admire her remarkable ability to look at my writing and ask the questions that would take it to the next level. Her insights and advice have truly made all the difference.

I was blessed to have literary agent Stephanie Tade jump aboard this adventure early on. She believed in my voice and my mission from the start. I could never find the words to thank the woman who knew, even before I did, that *Second Firsts* deserved to be published. Thank you, Stephanie.

I feel a sense of gratitude and love toward the publishing team at Hay House for their passion for my work and for inviting me to be part of their family. I still remember the first phone conversation I had with acquisitions director Patty Gift, where I felt as if we had known each other for a very long time. I'm thankful to senior editor Laura Gray for her insightful notes on the manuscript and her patience in guiding this first-time author through the publishing process. Laura arrived on this journey at the

very end, but her passion about my work and her ability to bend words, build bridges, and connect the dots have made this book flow in ways I never thought possible.

Thanks also to Nancy Levin, Hay House events director, for immediately making me feel special and at home; this was priceless to me.

I want to thank Allison Maslan for helping me see the value I had to offer to the world when I could not see it for myself. I am very grateful to the Royal Divas for their unconditional support and love throughout the year of writing: Robin Richter, Stephanie Gunning, Merideth Mehlberg, and LaNell Silverstein.

Thank you, Scott Tillitt of Antidote Collective, for seeing the value of the reentry model from the get-go; and Paulette Rao, M.C.C., B.C.C., of the Conscious Coaching Institute, for being the very first person to validate the phrase *Second Firsts*. She told me that I had to bring it into the world. I am forever thankful for that moment when she showed me her excitement for what this could be. My gratitude also extends to Pratt Bennett of Make that Leap, for helping me believe in the dream.

Melissa Samuelson Cassera of Cassera Communications has been a wonderful ally. Her passion for *Second Firsts* and for helping me bring it closer to my audience has been instrumental. I'm grateful to my right-hand girl, Carrie Ryan, for always listening, believing, and seeing the dream during the tough early days. I am also grateful for Cameron Ford's help in spreading the word about my book.

I am thankful for the support and love of the women of Rich, Happy & Hot B-School, Tribe 2011, for always being there to listen. Thank you, Marie Forleo, for always inspiring excellence. I could not have done this without them. I am thankful to Julie Cottineau for helping me think outside the box during her speech in New York City. I am grateful to Kay Lathrop for teaching me how to be a masterful coach through Results Coaching and for reading an early draft of portions of this book and believing in its power. I also have tremendous appreciation for the work of David Rock, founder of Neuroleadership Group, whose ideas have influenced me greatly. A special thank you to Alexandra Franzen for her ability to capture what was in my heart so easily and so accurately. My mission became more and more clear because of the mirror she was able to hold up for me over the years.

This book would not be possible without the bravehearted souls who allow me into their lives through my daily words, public programs, and coaching practice. By showing me that they were ready for something different, something that required action and renewed belief, these Life Starters inspired me with their eagerness to break out of the Waiting Room. This book came together to help them discover the doorway back to life. I am especially grateful to the very first Life Starters who subscribed to my newsletter, *Message in a Bottle,* and wrote back to me. Their support has carried me through my obstacles and fears. I believed in the importance of this material because of their love.

ABOUT THE AUTHOR

Christina Rasmussen is a strategist for life and business after loss. As the founder of Second Firsts, she's crusading to raise the bar of life after loss. As a coach and speaker, she's reaching individuals, professionals, and groups all over the world. SecondFirsts.com is her global coaching portal for reinvention and transformation. Her organization is devoted to helping people step out from the shadow of excruciating loss and come back to life. Christina serves anyone who has gone through a life-changing experience, such as divorce, death, severe illness, or job loss.

Christina is also the founder of TheLifeStarters.org, a nonprofit action-oriented social network for people who have been stuck in the Waiting Room after a life interruption and who do not have the money or the resources to get help.

Christina's personal story and fresh approach to life after loss has garnered international attention. Her blog articles have appeared on Huffington Post Impact, More, Life by Me, Hello Giggles, and KrisCarr.com. She's been featured as a Woman Working to Do Good in the White House Blog and was named a Leading Mom in Business by StartupNation.com.

Christina was born in Greece and has lived in England, Denmark, California, Texas, and Massachusetts. She taught herself fluent English over the course of four years while studying for her bachelor of arts degree in education and her master's degree in guidance and counseling at Durham University in England. After immigrating to the United States with her Danish husband in 1999, she earned a post-graduate certificate in human resources management from Northeastern University in Boston. She has been certified as a coach by David Rock's Results Coaching Systems and is a member of the International Coaching Federation.

Christina is the mother of two beautiful girls who watched their father die of cancer and saw their mother alchemize that tragedy into a new life for herself and others, a new marriage, a blended family, a renewed sense of purpose, and a lifestyle of joy and laughter. She resides in San Francisco, California, with her husband, Eric, their four daughters, and their dog, Tyson.

Hay House Titles of Related Interest

YOU CAN HEAL YOUR LIFE, the movie,
starring Louise L. Hay & Friends
(available as a 1-DVD program and an expanded 2-DVD set)
Watch the trailer at: www.LouiseHayMovie.com

THE SHIFT, the movie,
starring Dr. Wayne W. Dyer
(available as a 1-DVD program and an expanded 2-DVD set)
Watch the trailer at: www.DyerMovie.com

*DYING TO BE ME: My Journey from Cancer, to Near Death,
to True Healing,* by Anita Moorjani

*TAKE 2: Your Guide to Creating Happy Endings and
New Beginnings,* by Leeza Gibbons

WISHES FULFILLED: Mastering the Art of Manifesting,
by Dr. Wayne W. Dyer

All of the above are available at your local bookstore,
or may be ordered by contacting Hay House (see next page).

We hope you enjoyed this Hay House book. If you'd like to receive our online catalog featuring additional information on Hay House books and products, or if you'd like to find out more about the Hay Foundation, please contact:

Hay House, Inc., P.O. Box 5100, Carlsbad, CA 92018-5100
(760) 431-7695 or (800) 654-5126
(760) 431-6948 (fax) or (800) 650-5115 (fax)
www.hayhouse.com® • **www.hayfoundation.org**

Published and distributed in Australia by: Hay House Australia Pty. Ltd., 18/36 Ralph St., Alexandria NSW 2015 • *Phone:* 612-9669-4299 *Fax:* 612-9669-4144 • www.hayhouse.com.au

Published and distributed in the United Kingdom by: Hay House UK, Ltd., Astley House, 33 Notting Hill Gate, London W11 3JQ • *Phone:* 44-20-3675-2450 • *Fax:* 44-20-3675-2451 www.hayhouse.co.uk

Published and distributed in the Republic of South Africa by: Hay House SA (Pty), Ltd., P.O. Box 990, Witkoppen 2068 • *Phone/Fax:* 27-11-467-8904 • www.hayhouse.co.za

Published in India by: Hay House Publishers India, Muskaan Complex, Plot No. 3, B-2, Vasant Kunj, New Delhi 110 070 • *Phone:* 91-11-4176-1620 *Fax:* 91-11-4176-1630 • www.hayhouse.co.in

Distributed in Canada by: Raincoast, 9050 Shaughnessy St., Vancouver, B.C. V6P 6E5 • *Phone:* (604) 323-7100 • *Fax:* (604) 323-2600 www.raincoast.com

<u>Take Your Soul on a Vacation</u>

Visit **www.HealYourLife.com®** to regroup, recharge, and reconnect with your own magnificence. Featuring blogs, mind-body-spirit news, and life-changing wisdom from Louise Hay and friends.

Visit **www.HealYourLife.com** today!